MON'
BY LARRY AND NATHAN

RIVERBEND
PUBLISHING

**Cover photographs**
Front cover: Lodgepole Creek Falls; Back cover, top: Emerald Sun Falls;
Back cover, bottom, left to right: Rock Creek Falls, Ousel Falls, St. Mary
Falls

*Montana Waterfalls*
Copyright © 2011 by Larry and Nathan Johnson

Published by Riverbend Publishing, Helena, Montana

ISBN: 978-1-60639-033-7

Printed in China

1 2 3 4 5 6 7 8 9 0 EP 18 17 16 15 14 13 12 11

Cover design and page layout by Sarah E. Grant

Maps created using TOPO! software © 2001 National Geographic Maps.
To learn more visit: http://www.natgeomaps.com

Riverbend Publishing
P.O. Box 5833
Helena, MT 59604
1-866-787-2363
www.riverbendpublishing.com

**Disclaimer**
The authors and publisher do not assume and hereby disclaim any responsibility or liability for damages, losses, or injuries that might occur to those using the information in this book. Hiking and waterfall viewing all have potential hazards involving risk of injury or death. Although information in this book is intended to assist in locating waterfalls in Montana, it is neither represented nor guaranteed to be accurate or complete. Outdoor conditions change from day to day and season to season, rendering any information subject to change without warning. Those who use this information, and those who venture into the outdoors, do so at their own risk.

Additionally, some waterfalls or portions of routes described in this book may be on private land. Neither the authors nor the publisher encourage or authorize trespassing on private land and hereby disclaim any responsibility or liability for those doing so. It is the individual's responsibility to secure permission to travel on private land.

# CONTENTS

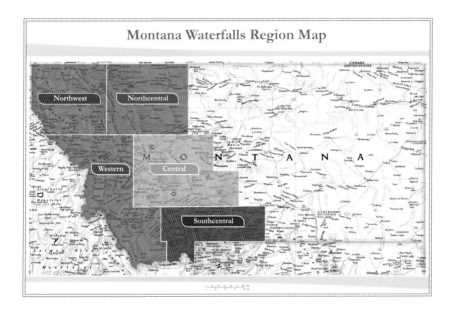

## Montana Waterfalls Region Map

MONTANA WATERFALLS BY REGIONS

# ACKNOWLEDGEMENTS

First we would like to express our gratitude to our publisher Chris Cauble, who has helped us immensely, our editor Barbara Fifer who did a great job with editing our text, our designer and the rest of the staff at Riverbend Publishing. Their enthusiasm and support for our book conveyed to us that it would be possible to publish a book on Montana Waterfalls.

Hello I'm Larry Johnson and this book has been a long journey that my son Nathan and I started on over seven years ago. Without the help and support and inspiration of many people along this quest, in my personal opinion, the writing of this book would not have been possible. To start with I want to thank my loving wife and friend Maria Elena, her parents Ezequiel and Maria, and the extended Benavides family especially David, Dan, Jeanne, Ruthanne, Edward and Uncle Bruce. I would also like to thank Nathan for all his hard work, technical skill and inspiration co-authoring this book, his good friend Elizabeth H. with her expertise in helping with our editing, and his son Tristan with his energy and enthusiasm made it a lot of fun. Many, many thanks to our daughter Yarrow, and her husband Mike and their two daughters Arabelle and Tia, whom at various times have hiked and camped with us on many of our excursions looking for waterfalls and enjoying the great outdoors. Also very special thanks to my mother Flo for inspiring me about the beauty of life and nature from the very beginning. Certainly growing up in a family that loved the outdoors was fortunate for me, so I want to personally thank my extended family, in particular Nancy, Brooke, Matthew, Stan, Sandy and Jim for their steadfast support. Finally, there are some good friends whom I would like to thank for their encouragement and interest in this project, so thanks Don M., Kathy, Don B., Colleen, Ron, Sheila, JoAnne, Phil, Dan S., Joanne S. and Roger.

Hi I'm Nathan Johnson and I have enjoyed immensely the adventures and rich relationships that creating this book has enabled me to experience. I would like to foremost give special thanks to my Dad for partnering in this endeavor with me. Second, I would like to thank my mom Vicki Varnum and my step dad Carl Godtland for their unending support, assistance and knowledge of Montana's history, Elizabeth Harrison for her pre-editing expertise, my son Tristan for his patience and positivity on many of our long drives, my step mom Maria for her unwavering support even when we were in the middle of nowhere faced with downpours, Yarrow and Mike Schmidt along with their two child bundles of energy – Tia and Arabelle, Tom Maley for his company during our long travels. I would also like to thank all of the Varnum family (John, Alice, Barbara and Elizabeth), The Burchnel family (Ann, Cooper, Copeland, Cy and Celeste), Michelle Adam, Emily Wyberg, Mike Atlas, Jessica Adam, Kathy, Don and Matthew May, Terri, Lynn and Cameron Fisher, Kevin Colburn, Nancy Tillemans, Jon Armendariz, Brooke Armendariz, Charlie Persson, John Geesen, John Macewicz and most importantly, the Creator of all that exists.

# INTRODUCTION

Welcome to the first edition of *Montana Waterfalls*. It has been a seven-year process in bringing our experiences, photos, and discoveries to you. We hope you enjoy the color, perspective, and awe we gleaned from our travels and gypsy caravans. The number and quality of waterfalls in Montana is staggering. In Glacier National Park alone, our rough estimate of wilderness quality waterfalls is well over a thousand. Many are still being discovered and shared.

The Wikipedia definition for a waterfall is a place where flowing water rapidly drops in elevation as it flows over a steep region or cliff. It goes on to say that waterfalls are considered one of the most beautiful phenomena in nature. That is what drove the two of us to search through countless maps, to go out in all seasons, driving to sometimes very remote areas of Montana, to hear, see, and discover this most beautiful phenomenon of nature.

There have been many times that we nestled into our tents, glowing with joy from yet another phenomenal discovery, whether it be a new falls, a hidden gorge, or a series of misting waterslides, only to be whisked away the next day to another eye-opener. Sometimes it was too much, like eating too many chocolate éclairs late at night without adult supervision. Other times, the experience of just being around the falling water was, at the very least, soul reviving. Sit quietly next to a waterfall and you will surely discover how meditative and calming the experience can be.

The diversity of Montana waterfalls is a result of geology. Much of the western and northwestern part of the state is overlain by very old — 900 million years and greater — sedimentary mudstones. This makes for a plethora of angular and sheer drops, depending on the tilt of the rock. Toward the center of the state and in parts of the western area are mountainous intrusions of granitic, volcanic, and metamorphic rocks supporting waterfalls that vary greatly in form. They range from twisting cascades following faults and fissures into emerald green pools, to bulbous, onion-layered granite waterslides flowing through multi-channeled micro-gorges.

Montana is a desirable place to live and much wealth and development has taken root here. If you are one of those lucky few to own property with access to a waterfall on public land, we encourage you to support public access to these precious resources.

As many of the indigenous tribes have said, "We do not inherit the Earth from our ancestors; we borrow it from our children."

"The earth is but one country and mankind its citizens"
— Baha'u'llah

— Larry and Nathan Johnson

# TERMS USED IN THIS BOOK

**Stream** is the body of water that the waterfall is located on. For this book, we researched U.S. Forest Service maps, Google Maps and DeLorme's *Montana Atlas & Gazetteer*.

**Size** is the size of the stream that holds the waterfall. Our categories are: small stream, creek, river, and large river.

**Watershed** is the major river drainage basin the said stream flows into. We have used 17 rivers to define watersheds in Montana Waterfalls.

**Height** is the approximate vertical distance in feet from a waterfall's base to its apex.

**Formation** is the shape or structure of a waterfall. We have listed nine formations to define the shape of the waterfall. Some waterfalls have more then one, and sometimes the formation will change depending on the current CFS (cubic feet of water flow per second) of the stream.

> **Cascade:** A series of water level drops over a rock surface descending downstream.

> **Gorge:** A steep, narrow ravine the stream pours through.

> **Horsetail:** A long narrow waterfall dropping almost vertically, but still is contact with bedrock, widening somewhat at the base.

> **Punchbowl:** A waterfall where the stream flows over an abrupt rock ledge straight down into a circular recirculating pool.

> **Sheer falls:** An almost perpendicular drop with the stream not in contact with the bedrock while descending.

> **Shoestring:** A long, slender, string-like waterfall that is intermittently in contact with the rock on its descent.

> **Slide:** A smooth continuous flow in contact with a bedrock surface that slants downward at about 45 degrees.

> **Terraced:** A wide, broader falls that can have a vertical drop or slant.

> **Tiered:** Two or more distinct separate levels of waterfalls, descending one after another.

**Elevation** is feet above sea level where the waterfall begins.

**Area** is one of the five regions we divided Montana into for this book. Our regions are Northwest, Western, Northcentral, Central, and Southcentral.

**County** is the Montana county where the waterfall is located.

**Forest** is usually the national forest or national park where a waterfall is located, unless otherwise noted.

**Hike** is the total length in miles from the trailhead to the waterfall and back to the trailhead. We have combined the length with a description of how difficult the hike is. There are 5 categories for difficulty: short walk from the road, easy hike, moderate hike, difficult hike, and hike with no defined trail, where a person must bushwhack to reach the waterfall.

**Road access** defines the type of road you drive to get to the waterfall or trailhead. We have used 4 classifications: Easy drive (direct highway access), dirt or gravel roads, rough road at times, and 4-wheel drive.

**Season** is the usual season(s) of the year best to view the waterfall.

**Latitude and Longitude** is the precise location of the waterfall. We have used Google Maps for our determination.

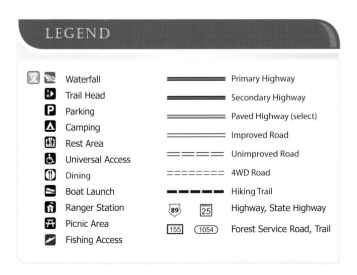

LEGEND

Waterfall — Primary Highway
Trail Head — Secondary Highway
Parking — Paved Highway (select)
Camping — Improved Road
Rest Area === Unimproved Road
Universal Access ======= 4WD Road
Dining — — — — Hiking Trail
Boat Launch
Ranger Station (89) [25] Highway, State Highway
Picnic Area
Fishing Access [155] (1054) Forest Service Road, Trail

Waterfalls can be dangerous. Take all necessary precautions around waterfalls and use common sense to stay safe. You are fully responsible for your own safety at all times. *Montana Waterfalls* uses four hazard icons to signify safety concerns at waterfalls.

 **Pedestrian danger—highway:** When hiking to or viewing the waterfall, you will be in close proximity to a highway.

 **Dangerous around the falls:** The area immediately around the waterfall has steep cliffs, abrupt drop-offs, unstable or slippery ground, etc.

 **Far from medical help:** Getting to the waterfall will place you far from medical help.

 **Grizzly bears:** This icon indicates that the waterfall is located in known grizzly bear country. Most of Montana's waterfalls are in bear country but not always grizzly country. Black bear encounters can be dangerous, but usually not to the level of grizzly bear encounters.

And if hiking:

- Do not trespass on private land. Always get permission before hiking on private land.

- Always let someone know where you are going and when you expect to be back.

- Take and know how to use maps and compasses, even if you use a GPS unit.

- Take and know how to use bear spray.

- Waterfalls and their environments are wet and slippery. Use good footwear and watch where you step.

 Each waterfall has a numerical "star" rating. These ratings are the authors' judgements about the beauty and impressiveness of each waterfall relative to other waterfalls, with one being the lowest rating and five being the highest. All the waterfalls in this book are rated two and higher.

# Montana Waterfalls Northwest Region

# Avalanche Creek Falls

## DESCRIPTION

Avalanche Gorge is a must-see destination for anyone in the West Glacier area. With its luscious green canopy of moss and brilliant red rocks, there is no wonder why this little gorge is a favorite place for photographers and travelers alike. At the falls near the bridge, the stream dives into an incredibly narrow chasm for about 40 feet. Some days, when the light is right, you can view rays of sunlight as they reach down into the gorge where the creek pours over small punch-bowl waterfalls.

*Avalanche Creek Gorge*

## SUMMARY

| | |
|---|---|
| **Stream**<br>• *Avalanche Creek* | **Watershed**<br>• *Flathead River* |
| **Size**<br>• *Creek* | **Forest**<br>• *Glacier National Park* |
| **Height**<br>• *15 ft.* | **Hike**<br>• *1.5 mi. - short walk from road* |
| **Formation**<br>• *Gorge* | **Road access**<br>• *Easy highway/road access* |
| **Elevation**<br>• *3434* | **Season**<br>• *Spring, Summer, Fall* |
| **Area**<br>• *Northwest* | **Latitude**<br>• *48.676709* |
| **County**<br>• *Flathead* | **Longitude**<br>• *-114.814626* |

### ACCESS

From West Glacier, drive north on Going-to-the-Sun Road for 16 miles to Avalanche Creek trailhead.

*Red baneberry is poisonous*

## HISTORY

Going-to-the-Sun Road is the main road driving through the park. It crosses the Continental Divide at the rugged grandeur of Logan Pass, elevation 6,468 feet. Construction on the road started in 1921 and was completed in 1932. It runs a distance of 54.8 miles from West Glacier to East Glacier, and was one of the very first roads built by the National Park Service for the purpose of automobile tourist traffic. In 1983, Going-to-the-Sun Road was added to the National Register of Historic Places.

Trail of the Cedars is located next to Avalanche Creek Campground. This wheelchair-accessible trail is a loop that starts out from the parking lot. It is a nicely constructed boardwalk on the north side of Avalanche Creek and a paved asphalt trail on the south side. There are many interpretive signs along the path, which winds through towering old-growth cedar and hemlock trees.

*Avalanche Creek Gorge*

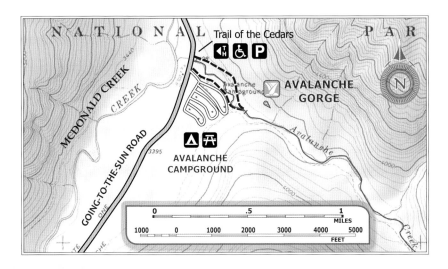

## CAMPING

**Avalanche Campground** is located within tall, old-growth hemlock and western red cedar trees. This campground accommodates both tents and RVs, with 87 sites available. There are also potable water, handicapped-accessible toilet facilities and a $15 per day fee. For hikers, there are a couple of scenic trails starting out of Avalanche campground: Trail of the Cedars and Avalanche Lake. During the summer, there are many evening programs with National Park Service rangers at the Avalanche Amphitheater.

**Sprague Creek Campground** is situated off the northeast shore of Lake McDonald. This is a relatively small campground of 25 sites that operates on a first-come first-served basis. Potable water is available, along with flush toilets and sinks with running water. It also has a very nice picnic area, and about a mile away, at the historic Lake McDonald Lodge, boat tours are available.

**Glacier National Park**
P.O. Box 128
West Glacier, MT 59936
406-888-7800

## DESCRIPTION

There is no known trail up to Bird Woman Falls, and bushwhacking from the bottom up Logan Creek would be extremely difficult. Below the Weeping Wall, along Going-to-the-Sun Road, numerous scenic overlooks offer unobstructed views of Bird Woman Falls with Mount Cannon and Mount Oberlin in the backdrop. These overlooks are located on Logan Pass where Glacier Route 1 (also known as Going-to-the-Sun Road) runs over the Continental Divide and down to the eastern side of the park.

*Bird Woman Falls*

## SUMMARY

| | |
|---|---|
| **Stream**<br>• *South Fork of Logan Creek* | **Watershed**<br>• *Flathead River* |
| **Size**<br>• *Small stream* | **Forest**<br>• *Glacier National Park* |
| **Height**<br>• *492 ft.* | **Hike**<br>• *none* |
| **Formation**<br>• *Shoestring* | **Road access**<br>• *Easy highway/road access* |
| **Elevation**<br>• *5863* | **Season**<br>• *Summer, Fall* |
| **Area**<br>• *Northwest* | **Latitude**<br>• *48.707672* |
| **County**<br>• *Flathead* | **Longitude**<br>• *-113.747892* |

### ACCESS

From West Glacier take Glacier Route 1 northwest 14.5 miles to the scenic overlooks for Bird Woman Falls.

*Bighorn ram near falls*

## HISTORY

Glacier Park celebrated its 100th year anniversary in 2010. The park was established on May 11, 1910, as the nation's 10th national park. Evidence of early aboriginal peoples living along the eastern front of the Rockies goes back 10,000 years or more. The present-day Blackfeet, Salish and Kootenai tribes of Montana arrived later, possibly in the 1700s. The Blackfeet migrated from the Great Lakes area of Ontario and Manitoba, whereas the Salish and Kootenai arrived from the area of Washington and British Columbia.

Spanish, English and French trappers in search of beaver pelts started appearing on the stage in the early 1800s and by the mid- to late 1800s, homesteaders and miners had pushed into Montana forcing the remaining native tribes onto reservations.

No long after the turn of the century, a character known as George Bird Grinnell recognized the invaluable treasure and beauty of the area and with help of a few folks was able to help persuade President Taft to establish a national park.

*Siyeh limestone on Granite Park Tr.*

*Flowers on Granite Park Trail*

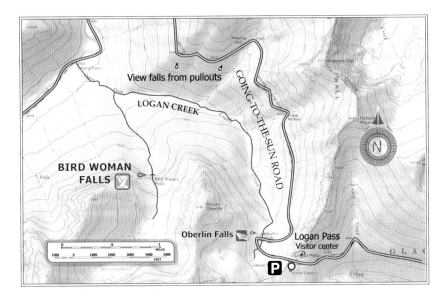

## CAMPING

**Rising Sun Campground** is 6.2 miles west from the St. Mary entrance along the historic Going-to-the-Sun Road. It is located just off of St. Marys Lake and is noted for its incredibly scenic views. There are 83 sites that are first-come, first- serve. The campground has potable water, sinks with running water, showers and flush toilets. Nightly evening programs hosted by a park ranger are held at the campground amphitheater. There is a camp store adjacent to the campground, and St. Marys Lake offers boat tours.

**Avalanche Campground** is located within tall, old-growth hemlock and western red cedar trees. This campground accommodates both tents and RVs, with 87 sites available. There is also potable water, handicapped-accessible toilet facilities and a $15 per day fee. For hikers, there are a couple of popular scenic trails starting out of Avalanche campground: Trail of the Cedars and Avalanche Lake. During the summer there are many evening programs with National Park rangers at the Avalanche Amphitheater.

Glacier National Park
P.O. Box 128
West Glacier, MT 59936
406-888-7800

# Graves Creek Falls

## DESCRIPTION

The trail leading to the top of Graves Creek Falls starts from the pull-through parking area. From the start of the trail to the falls is only 200 yards. Walking the trail, you're flanked by bracken ferns off the side and Douglas-fir overhead. Lush plant growth greets you as the trail opens up to the sight of a misty slide-like falls. The top half speeds down an incredible ramp ,while the lower half slides into a blue-green pool.

*Graves Creek*

| | |
|---|---|
| **Stream** <br> • Graves Creek | **Watershed** <br> • Clark Fork |
| **Size** <br> • Creek | **Forest** <br> • Lolo National Forest |
| **Height** <br> • 95 ft. | **Hike** <br> • 0.1 mi. - short walk from road |
| **Formation** <br> • Slide | **Road access** <br> • Dirt roads |
| **Elevation** <br> • 2949 | **Season** <br> • Spring, Summer and Fall |
| **Area** <br> • Western | **Latitude** <br> • 47.720849 |
| **County** <br> • Sanders | **Longitude** <br> • -115.378032 |

## ACCESS

From Thompson Falls drive north on Montana Highway 200 for 1.1 to Montana Secondary 472 (Blue Slide Road). Turn right onto Blue Slide Road and drive 6.4 miles to Graves Creek Road. Turn right onto Graves Creek Road and drive up it for 2.8 miles to a small parking area for the trailhead, which is to the left.

*Alpine sunflower*

## HISTORY

Thompson Falls was named after David Thompson (1770-1857) a British-born Canadian, surveyor, explorer, geographer and fur trader. While working for North West Company he founded the Saleesh House in 1809 at the location of present-day Thompson Falls. The Saleesh House was the first trading post west of the Continental Divide in Montana. Thompson's 1797-1798 expedition map, produced while surveying and mapping the upper Mississippi River (Missouri) headwaters, was incorporated into a map Lewis and Clark used on their historic journey. David Thompson is credited with surveying and mapping over his career some 3.9 million square kilometers of wilderness.

## CAMPING

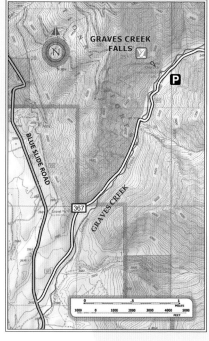

**North Shore Campground** (USFS elevation 2,200') is located on the shore of Noxon Reservoir one mile off Montana Highway 200 some two miles west of Trout Creek. There are 13 campsites available from April 15 to November 30. It has potable water, handicapped accessible toilets and a boat ramp for access onto Noxon Reservoir.

Kootenai National Forest
31374 US Highway 2
Libby, MT 59923-3022
406-293-6211

**Thompson Falls State Park** (Montana Fish, Wildlife and Parks) is a shaded, peaceful campground located off the banks of the Clarks Fork River (Elevation 2,362'). This campground is one mile northwest of Thompson Falls on Montana Highway 200. This is a packin–packout campground with potable water, handicapped accessible toilets, handicapped accessible fishing area and a small boat launch that is open from May 1st to September 30th.

Montana Fish, Wildlife & Parks
Parks Division
406-444-3750

## DESCRIPTION

You will fall in love with this place. The Jewel Basin is just to the west, Hungry Horse Reservoir to the east, Handkerchief Lake, innumerable waterfalls and some nice campsites will more than entice you to come back. Graves Creek Falls is just upstream from the bridge that crosses the road with the small trail heading upstream from a small pullout picnic area. Below the bridge, the creek flows into the reservoir but not before careening off one last glistening cascade. A mile above Handkerchief Lake you'll find a pull out in the road displaying Sun and Moon Falls, a nearly sheer drop surrounded by low-hanging brush. This section of the creek has recently been discovered as a high quality but very difficult kayaking run. Hiking from the trailhead just up the road from Sun and Moon Falls will bring you to a series of waterfalls and cascades, in fact more than you can count. Be sure to explore these. Have fun!

*Graves Creek Falls*

## SUMMARY

| | |
|---|---|
| **Stream**<br>• Graves Creek | **Watershed**<br>• Flathead River |
| **Size**<br>• Small stream | **Forest**<br>• Flathead National Forest |
| **Height**<br>• 35 ft. | **Hike**<br>• 0.4 mi. - short walk from road |
| **Formation**<br>• Terraced | **Road access**<br>• Dirt roads |
| **Elevation**<br>• 3580 | **Season**<br>• Spring, Summer and Fall |
| **Area**<br>• Northwest | **Latitude**<br>• 48.126808 |
| **County**<br>• Flathead | **Longitude**<br>• -113.810513 |

From Hungry Horse drive south on the West Side Road (Forest Road 895) 33.6 miles to NFDR 9796. Turn right onto NFDR 9796 and drive 1.0 miles to NFDR 897. Turn right onto NFDR 9796 and drive 300 yards to a small parking area on the left next to Graves Creek.

*Western trillium*

## HISTORY

Hungry Horse Dam was completed in 1953 and is 564 feet high. Hungry Horse Reservoir is 34 miles long covering an area of almost 24,000 acres. It is named after an incident that happened during the winter of 1900-1901, when two freight horses wandered away up the South Fork of the Flathead River. They were found a month later in deep snow, starving and weak. The story goes that they were able to be slowly nursed back to health. The name stuck in the area—along with the the dam and reservoir, there are Hungry Horse Creek, Hungry Horse Mountain and the community of Hungry Horse.

*Sun and Moon Falls*

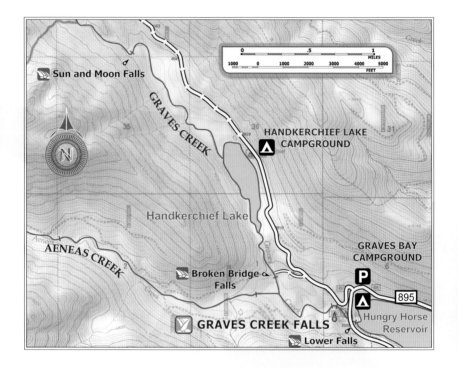

## CAMPING

**Handkerchief Lake Campground** (USFS, elevation 3,858') is in the Flathead National Forest 35 miles south of Hungry Horse, about 1 mile from Hungry Horse Reservoir. This is a small pack in–pack out campground with 9 campsites available. It has one vault toilet and access to serene, 32-acre Handkerchief Lake. Maximum stay limit is 14 days.

Flathead National Forest
650 Wolfpack Way
Kalispell, MT 59901
406-758-5200

# Kootenai Falls

## DESCRIPTION

Kootenai Falls is one of the few large waterfalls along a major Northwest river that has not been harnessed for electrical power. Nestled in the Cabinet Mountains, the falls drop around 200 feet in an almost unspoiled setting. The trailhead starts at Kootenai Falls County Park, sitting in a shady cedar grove, located just off US Highway 2. There are a picnic area and restrooms, along with interpretive signs. The trail to the falls is narrow, crossing railroad tracks via an overpass. A quarter of a mile farther along, the trail splits, with the right fork going to the falls another 1/4 mile away. An adventurous hiker can go down the left fork of the trail to the Kootenai River Gorge and walk across a swinging bridge. Looking south across the Kootenai River, you get an impressive view of the Cabinet Mountain Wilderness

*Kootenai Falls in January*

| Stream | Watershed |
|--------|-----------|
| • *Kootenai River* | • *Kootenai River* |
| **Size** | **Forest** |
| • *Large river* | • *Kootenai National Forest* |
| **Height** | **Hike** |
| • *75 ft.* | • *1.5 mi. - Easy hike* |
| **Formation** | **Road access** |
| • *Terraced* | • *Easy highway/road access* |
| **Elevation** | **Season** |
| • *1969* | • *All* |
| **Area** | **Latitude** |
| • *Northwest* | • *48.455136* |
| **County** | **Longitude** |
| • *Lincoln* | • *-115.764227* |

### ACCESS

From Troy, travel east on US Highway 2 for 6.8 miles to Kootenai Falls County Park. The trailhead that leads down to the falls starts at the back end of the park, away from the highway.

### HISTORY

The Kootenai River flows out of Canada from several pristine tributaries as the Elk, St. Mary and Bull rivers. The water, which is usually a brilliant turquoise blue, is colored from the residues and deposits of the steady carving of glaciers located primarilyin its British Columbia headwaters. The river makes its way through Lake Koocanusa, takes an abrupt ninety-degree turn and heads west on its destination to the Pacific. It flows quietly until it reaches the terraced bedrock of Kootenai Falls, where it plummets forty feet over one of the Northwest's highest-volume waterfalls. It is a marvelous and dramatic sight. The main falls is so wide that one can barely see the details of falls near the right-hand bank. After the initial drop the river splits around an island. The right channel, which is unseen from the left bank, tumbles over a twenty-foot drop called Tahiti Falls.

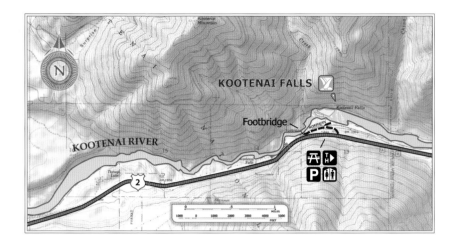

## CAMPING

**Fireman's Park** on US Highway 2 west is provided by the City of Libby, Montana. Camping fees are $5/day for RV's and $2/day for tents. There is a five-day camping limit, with tables, potable water, and restrooms available.

**Dorr Skeels Campground** (USFS) is on State Highway 56 south 13 miles of the junction US 2 and MH 56. Located next to Bull Lake at 2300' elevation in a great mountain setting, this is nice little Kootenai National Forest campground. There are but 3 camping units, no fee, tables, fire pits, potable water, vaulted restrooms and a boat ramp at Dorr Skeels.

**Bad Medicine Campground** (USFS) is reached by driving 15 miles west of Libby Montana on US Highway 2 to State Highway 56. Turn south for 21 miles to Ross Creek Cedars road. Go west for 2 miles to Bad Medicine Campground. There are 17 camping units, $10/day fee, tables, grated fire-pots, potable water, vaulted restrooms, with a 14 day maximum stay limit.

Kootenai National Forest
31374 US Highway 2
Libby, MT 59923-3022
406-293-6211

# Lost Johnny Creek Falls
## NORTHWEST MONTANA

## DESCRIPTION

If you're down with a short, rewarding, but ego-busting bush-whack, then this one is for you. There is no trail or even trace of one save the skid-marks your shoes will make while attempting to escape the small forest of devils club after you have lost your glasses. Some say, mistakenly, that grabbing devils club and thinking it be a friendly hand up over a log is worse than getting the date for your wedding day wrong. However it pans out for you, head toward the roaring sound of the creek. When you get to the creek, notice that the farther down you go the bigger the cascade gets until is flows over a near verti-cal falls of about 50 feet. This is the meat of Lost Johnny Falls. In total it's nearly 300 feet long! Happy thrashing.

*Lost Johnny Creek Falls*

## SUMMARY

| | |
|---|---|
| **Stream**<br>• Lost Johnny Creek | **Watershed**<br>• Flathead River |
| **Size**<br>• Creek | **Forest**<br>• Flathead National Forest |
| **Height**<br>• 140 ft. | **Hike**<br>• 0.4 mi. - Bushwack |
| **Formation**<br>• Terraced | **Road access**<br>• Dirt roads |
| **Elevation**<br>• 4131 | **Season**<br>• Spring, Summer and Fall |
| **Area**<br>• Northwest | **Latitude**<br>• 46.223226 |
| **County**<br>• Flathead | **Longitude**<br>• -113.039746 |

## ACCESS

From Hungry Horse, head south on the West Side Road (FR 895) for 9.2 miles to FR 895B. Turn left onto FR 895B, driving parallel with Lost Johnny Creek for 1.7 miles to a pullout next to the road. The bushwhack starts here and heads down to the creek. If you drive too far you will be able to see the creek and the road will flatten out somewhat.

*Hungry Horse Dam and Bob Marshall Wilderness*

## HISTORY

Just to the southwest and over the ridge line of Lost Johnny Creek are areas that vast glaciers around 15,000 years ago carved southward, splitting where present-day Big Fork sits. The west-side glacier carved out what is now Flathead Lake and its east-side twin rumbled down the Swan Valley, spooning out the landscape like a giant ice cream scoop. Just south of Big Fork the Mission Mountains begin to rise. Near the town and for a ways south they are low and rounded, perhaps due to glaciation riding up on the root of the mountains. Farther south, the Missions rise to much greater heights, then are abruptly cut off by the St. Mary fault.

*Little Falls, one mile upstream*

## CAMPING

**Lost Johnny Camp Campground** USFS) is 9 miles south of Hungry Horse. It's a pack in–pack out campground with 5 csites available, vaulted restrooms, potable water, fishing access and a $13/day fee. Lost Johnny Point Campground (USFS, elevation 3,606') is on the shore impressive 34-mile-long Hungry Horse Reservoir. There are 21 campsites available, potable water and wheelchair accessible restrooms. There also is a fishing access and boat launch access for a $13/day campground fee.

Flathead National Forest
Hungry Horse District
10 Hungry Horse Drive
Hungry Horse, MT 59919

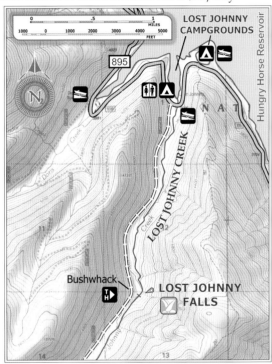

## DESCRIPTION

The trail starts at the west end of the parking area. Kootenai National Forest has built a nice graded handicapped accessible trail to the falls. Western red cedar, Engelmann spruce and subalpine fir line the banks of the West Fork of the Yaak River as you walk parallel to it. After a short hike of 500 yards you come to the observation deck that overlooks magnificent Lower Falls.

*Lower Falls Yaak River*

SUMMARY

| | |
|---|---|
| **Stream** <br> • *West Fork of the Yaak River* | **Watershed** <br> • *Yaak River* |
| **Size** <br> • *River* | **Forest** <br> • *Kootenai National Forest* |
| **Height** <br> • *25 ft.* | **Hike** <br> • *1.5 mi. - Easy hike* |
| **Formation** <br> • *Tiered* | **Road access** <br> • *Dirt roads* |
| **Elevation** <br> • *3514* | **Season** <br> • *Spring, Summer and Fall* |
| **Area** <br> • *Northwest* | **Latitude** <br> • *48.929492* |
| **County** <br> • *Lincoln* | **Longitude** <br> • *-115.723414* |

### ACCESS

From Yaak, drive east on National Forest Development Road (Yaak River Road) 6.7 miles to NFDR 92. Turn left onto NFDR 92, driving west 2.4 miles to NFDR 276. Turn left on NFDR 276, traveling 2.3 miles to National Forest Development Road 5857. Turn onto NFDR 5857, going another 0.5 mile to the parking lot and the trailhead.

*Hobbits in search of falling water*

### HISTORY

The Great Burn (or Great Fire) of 1910 started on August 20, 1910. The firestorm burned for only two days, but after this historical blowup over 3 million acres were burned—an area the size of the state of Connecticut. It is now believed to be the largest fire ever recorded in the United States. This fire burned parts of 3 states and 10 national forests. It is notable that, after this fire and the other approximately 3,000 forest fires that summer, Congress in 1911 authorized the first forest-fire protection plan.

*Upper Falls Yaak River*

## CAMPING

**Red Top Campground** (USFS) is a nice forested campground just up off the Yaak River, adjacent to Red Top Creek. From the junction of US Highway 2 and the Yaak River Road, it's about 25 miles to the campsite, a pack in–pack out site with 5 camping units and a vaulted toilet. This Kootenai National Forest campground is open year around and managed from May 15 to September 10 with a 14-day stay limit. No fee.

**Whitetail Campground** (USFS) is next to the alluring Yaak River 6.9 miles from the community of Yaak. Amid a dense green forest are 12 campsites. The campground has potable water, handicapped accessible restroom and an undeveloped boat ramp with access to the Yaak River. Whitetail is open year-round and managed with a campground host from May 15 through September 10. Fee is $7.00/night.

Kootenai National Forest
31374 US Highway 2
Libby, MT 59923-3022
(406) 293-6211

# Martin Falls

## DESCRIPTION

As you pull into the small parking area for Martin Falls, you will notice that it is surrounded by a healthy forest of subalpine fir, western red cedar and western hemlock. The forest floor is a rich, heavy undergrowth of bracken and mountain woodfern, maple liverwort, and wet-rock moss mixed into thick duff. The undeveloped trail leads you to magical Martin Falls a mere 50 feet away.

*Martin Falls*

SUMMARY

| | |
|---|---|
| **Stream** <br> • Martin Creek | **Watershed** <br> • Flathead River |
| **Size** <br> • Creek | **Forest** <br> • Flathead National Forest |
| **Height** <br> • 55 ft. | **Hike** <br> • 0.25 mi.-short walk from road |
| **Formation** <br> • Cascade | **Road access** <br> • Dirt roads |
| **Elevation** <br> • 3842 | **Season** <br> • Spring, Summer and Fall |
| **Area** <br> • Northwest | **Latitude** <br> • 48.565589 |
| **County** <br> • Flathead | **Longitude** <br> • -114.682975 |

ACCESS

From Olney, go west on Good Creek Road for 0.6 mile to the Martin Camp Road. Go straight on Martin Camp Road for 0.7 mile. Merge onto National Forest Development Road 60 and continue for 1.7 miles to Martin Creek Road (NFDR 910). Turn right onto Martin Creek Road for 4.7 miles, where on the left is a small parking area for the trailhead surrounded by towering cedar and hemlock trees.

*Brown-eyed susan*

### HISTORY

The name for the Tobacco Valley, which runs from the Canadian border north of Eureka down to almost Olney, most historians agree, comes from a native plant that the local Indians grew from seed, which closely resembled commercial tobacco. This happened to be quite popular, as the names Tobacco River, Tobacco Plains (the original name for Eureka) and Tobacco Prairie attest. David Thompson, the world-famous cartographer and explorer, in 1808 documented passing through the area on his journey seeking a water passage to the Pacific Ocean. From 1853 to1854 a survey expedition led by Caption John Mullan came through, laying out a wagon and railroad route from Fort Benton on the Missouri River to Walla Walla on the Columbia River. This route was to become known as the Mullan Road.

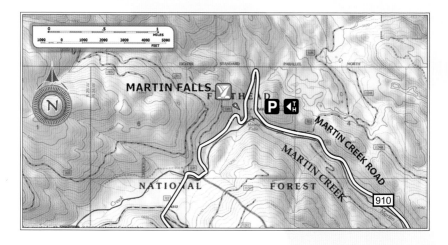

### CAMPING

**North Dickey Lake Campground** (USFS elevation 3,100') is south of Fortine by 4.2 miles, and located on the north shore of a very attractive, clean-watered lake. This forested campground has 25 camp-sites, handicapped accessible toilets and potable water. It also has a nice swimming beach and boat facilities.

Flathead National Forest
650 Wolfpack Way
Kalispell, MT 59901
406-758-5200

# McDonald Falls

## DESCRIPTION

This is the quintessential playtime sandbox for the gawking masses. Tourists gather against the short, hand-made rock wall to get a brief glimpse of Glacier Park paradise. McDonald Falls is a wide, powerful falls and well worth taking the little trail down a bit farther for a better look. The far side (west) of the creek offers better views. To hike to the falls this way, access the easy tree-lined trail from the bridge just downstream.

McDonald Creek Trail begins at the small parking area for the trailhead just a couple of hundred yards from Park Ranger Station at the north end of McDonald Lake. The trail winds through a heavily forested section somewhat away from McDonald Creek. After about a quarter of a mile, the trail comes closer to the creek. At that point you will have to bushwhack the last 100 yards in order to get a better view of powerful, roaring McDonald Falls. Back at the Mission Creek Trail, if you decide to continue hiking towards Sacred Dancing Cascade, at 0.4 mile you will come to a trail junction. To the right is a footbridge that crosses McDonald Creek just downstream from Sacred Dancing Cascade and goes to a parking area. The McDonald Creek Trail continues along the north side of the creek past Sacred Dancing Cascades.

*McDonald Falls*

SUMMARY

| Stream | Watershed |
|--------|-----------|
| • McDonald Creek | • Flathead River |
| **Size** | **Forest** |
| • Creek | • Glacier National Park |
| **Height** | **Hike** |
| • 35 ft. | • 0.9 mi. - Easy hike |
| **Formation** | **Road access** |
| • Terraced | • Easy highway/road access |
| **Elevation** | **Season** |
| • 3232 | • Summer, Fall |
| **Area** | **Latitude** |
| • Northwest | • 48.6398 |
| **County** | **Longitude** |
| • Flathead | • -113.864579 |

From Apgar Campground drive north on Going-to-the-Sun Road 9.5 miles to North Lake McDonald Road. Turn left on North Lake McDonald Road and go 0.3 miles, crossing over McDonald Creek bridge then on to the trailhead parking area off to the right.

*Sacred Dancing Cascade*

## HISTORY

Lake McDonald Lodge is a rustic three-and-a-half-story Swiss chalet–style building, with clipped gables, upper floor balconies, and Old World detailing. A land speculator, John E. Lewis, purchased the property in 1906. In 1913 Lewis had an architectural firm, Kirkland, Cutter, and Malmgren from Spokane, Washington, design the historical hotel.

The Lewis Glacier Hotel opened for business on June 14, 1914. Ownership changed hands in 1930, when a subsidiary of the Great Northern Railway, the Glacier Park Hotel Company, bought the hotel. The name was changed to Lake McDonald Lodge in 1957. Lake McDonald Lodge was listed May 28, 1987 on the National Register of Historic Places.

*Near Heaven's Peak*

## CAMPING

**Apgar Campground** (NPS) with 194 campsites it is the biggest campground in Glacier National Park. Located at the south end of Lake McDonald (elevation 3,143'). Available are potable water, flush toilets and sinks with running water. Evening programs with a park ranger are held at the Apgar Amphitheater during the summer season (May 8 to October 12).

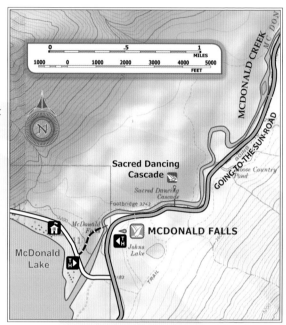

**Sprague Creek Campground** is situated off the northeast shore of Lake McDonald. This is a relatively small campground of 25 sites that operates on first-come first-served basis. There is potable water available, along with flush toilets and sinks with running water. It also has a very nice picnic area and about a mile away, at the historic Lake McDonald Lodge, boat tours of the lake are offered.

Glacier National Park
P.O. Box 128
West Glacier, MT 59936
406-888-7800

## DESCRIPTION

Do you like bears? Do bears like waterfalls? Let's hope your relationship to both is long and happy. Yes, there are bears in the Mission Mountains and yes, grizzlies. It's a good thing that in general, bears enjoy huckleberries more than pursuing people. The falls, however, will make great company as you sit near its 20', water-worn plunge. From the trailhead, hike about 0.75 mile to where the trail climbs a bit and settles on a bench. Follow the bench down to the creek, all the while listening for the roar of the falls. It's a good idea to make a racket; bears don't like to be surprised. Make noise and have some fun, right?

*North Crow Creek Falls*

SUMMARY

| Stream | Watershed |
|---|---|
| • North Crow Creek | • Flathead River |
| **Size** | **Forest** |
| • Creek | • Confederated Salish & Kootenai Tribes |
| **Height** | **Hike** |
| • 22 ft. | • 2 mi. - Easy hike |
| **Formation** | **Road access** |
| • Punchbowl | • Dirt Roads |
| **Elevation** | **Season** |
| • 5194 | • Spring, Summer and Fall |
| **Area** | **Latitude** |
| • Northwest | • 47.577302 |
| **County** | **Longitude** |
| • Lake | • -113.997409 |

## ACCESS

From Ronan head north on US Highway 93 for 0.7 mile to Old US Highway 93. Turn right onto Old US Highway 93 for 1.4 miles to Canyon Mill Road. Turn right onto Canyon Mill Road for 3.6 miles to North Crow Road. Take another right onto North Crow Road for 1.3 miles to the end at North Crow Creek Campground.

*Mission Mountains south of falls*

## HISTORY

Spring Creek started in 1883 as a small trading post settlement. In 1885, with the development of a new sawmill and a flour mill, the town's name was changed to Ronan Springs in honor of the local Indian agent Peter Ronan. When a post office was added in 1894, the name became simply Ronan. In August 1912, a fire broke out at an automobile garage, and burned the entire town except for four buildings.

There is an interesting legend of a gargantuan gold deposit located around this area. The story has it that a local found a gold vein nearly 1 foot thick and 100 feet long, near the tree line of a mountain just north of the falls. He supposedly took a fist-sized nugget from the vein, brought it home and showed his family and close friends. The following day he went back to the location and blasted the cliff above the vein, burying and hiding it from other miners. When he got back to town he began to assemble a crew to extract the ore, but died just before showing his crew the exact location of the gold. To this day no trace of gold has been found in the area, but strange hints like a ridge called "Minesinger" (which could refer to a German singing tradition and not a mine) and a group of closed mining claims nearby support curiosity within the circles of those afflicted with gold fever.

Flathead Lake was first recorded by the Canadian explorer David Thompson in his journal in 1812. This is a naturally formed lake some 30 miles long and 16 miles wide, over 300' deep, covering 191.5 square miles—with the Flathead River and Swan River as its two main tributaries. In 1885 the steamship U.S. Grant began hauling freight and passengers to the small communities around the shore. Today the area is known for its mild climate, its many recreational opportunities and its incredible beauty.

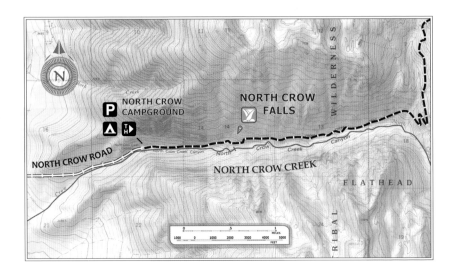

## CAMPING

**North Crow Creek Campground** (CSKT) has 2 campsites available. The campground has a restroom and there is fishing access to North Crow Creek.

**McDonald Lake Campground** (CSKT, elevation 3,642′) has 4 campsites. There are restrooms, fishing access and a boat launch access to McDonald Lake.

Confederated Salish & Kootenai Tribes
42487 Complex Blvd.
P.O. Box 278
Pablo, MT 59855
406-675-2700

## DESCRIPTION

A short hike down a densely wooded hillside puts you near the base of Vermillion Falls. The terraced formation is typical of many falls in northwestern Montana, especially those sedimentary formations lying horizontally. In the case of Vermillion Falls, its sedimentary rocks are of the Belt Series. The cascades and whitewater continue for a mile or so beyond the falls. You might be able to catch a glimpse of these from the road downstream.

*Vermillion Falls*

SUMMARY

| Stream | Watershed |
|---|---|
| • Vermillion River | • Clark Fork River |
| **Size** | **Forest** |
| • River | • Lolo National Forest |
| **Height** | **Hike** |
| • 34 ft. | • 0.2 mi. - short walk from road |
| **Formation** | **Road access** |
| • Terraced | • Dirt roads |
| **Elevation** | **Season** |
| • 3428 | • Spring, Summer and Fall |
| **Area** | **Latitude** |
| • Northwest | • 47.879398 |
| **County** | **Longitude** |
| • Sanders | • -115.355158 |

## ACCESS

From Thompson Falls, drive west on Montana Highway 200 for 22.6 miles to Blue Slide Road. Turn right onto Blue Slide Road (Vermillion River Road), driving east for 15.2 miles to the pullout/parking area for the falls.

Millipede

## HISTORY

In 1867, prospectors traveling to or from the many boom towns that had sprung up in Montana, found gold on the Vermillion River a few miles upstream from its confluence with the Clark Fork River.

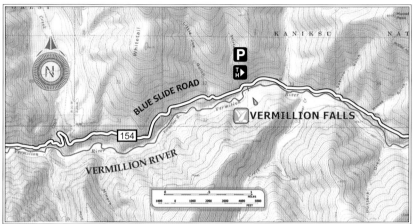

## CAMPING

**North Shore Campground** (USFS elevation 2,200') is located on the shore of Noxon Reservoir one mile off Montana Highway 200 and some two miles west of Trout Creek. There are 13 campsites available from April 15 to November 30. It has potable water, handicapped accessible toilets and a boat ramp for access to Noxon Reservoir.

Kootenai National Forest
31374 US Highway 2
Libby, MT 59923-3022
(406) 293-6211

**Thompson Falls State Park** (Montana Fish, Wildlife and Parks) is a shaded, peaceful campground located off the banks of the Clarks Fork River (elevation 2,362'). This campground is one mile northwest of Thompson Falls on Montana Highway 200. The campground is pack in–pack out, with potable water, handicapped accessible toilets, handicapped accessible fishing area and a small boat launch that is open from May 1 to September 30.

Montana Fish, Wildlife & Parks
Parks Division
406-444-3750

# Yaak Falls

## DESCRIPTION

Yaak Falls, with the Kootenai National Forest as its background, tumbles down a glimmering bedrock surface of green Precambrian mudstone. In high-water season, the river powers down this ramp and crashes into a wall—sending a plume of water 15 feet skyward. The undeveloped trailhead starts at the back of the campground and is just a short, 0.25-mile hike up to the falls.

*Yaak Falls upper portion*

*Yaak Falls lower portion*

SUMMARY

| | |
|---|---|
| **Stream**<br>• Yaak River | **Watershed**<br>• Kootenai River |
| **Size**<br>• River | **Forest**<br>• Kootenai National Forest |
| **Height**<br>• 50 ft. | **Hike**<br>• 0.1 mi. - short walk from road |
| **Formation**<br>• Slide | **Road access**<br>• Easy highway/road access |
| **Elevation**<br>• 2448 | **Season**<br>• All |
| **Area**<br>• Northwest | **Latitude**<br>• 48.648732 |
| **County**<br>• Lincoln | **Longitude**<br>• -115.885162 |

**ACCESS**

From Troy, drive west on US Highway 2, paralleling the awesome Kootenai River, and travel 10.4 miles to the Yaak River Road. Turn north on Montana State Secondary Highway 508 (Yaak River Road), then go 6.2 miles to Yaak River Campground. Turn right into the campground, and go on to its northeast corner, from which an undeveloped trail leads to the falls.

*Shooting stars along Yaak River*

## HISTORY

Yaak Falls is named after the Yaak Indian tribe who once popu-
lated this remote part of Montana. The ancient exposed Belt Series
rock is dated somewhere between 850 million and 1.5 billion years old.
The Great Fire (also Great Burn) of 1910 started on August 20, 1910. The
firestorm burned for only two days, but after this historical blowup over
3 million acres were burned. Affecting an area the size of the state of
Connecticut, it is now believed to be the largest fire ever recorded in the
United States. This fire burned parts of 3 states and 10 national forests.
It is notable that, after this fire and the other approximately 3,000 forest
fires that summer, Congress in 1911 authorized the first forest fire protection plan.

## CAMPING

**Yaak Falls
Campground**
is a really sweet
little pack in–pack
out campground
that is nestled in
a natural conifer
forest setting. There
are seven campsites
with a maximum
stay of 14 days,
offering toilets, no
drinking water and
no camping fee.

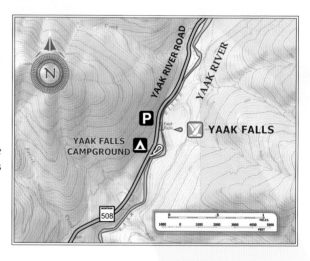

**Red Top Campground** (USFS) is a nice forested campground just off
the Yaak River, adjacent to Red Top Creek. From the junction of US
Highway 2 and the Yaak River Road, it's about 25 miles to the campsite.
This is a pack in–pack out site with 5 camping units and a vaulted toilet.
This Kootenai National Forest campground is open year around and
managed from May 15 to September 10, with a 14-day stay limit. No fee.

Kootenai National Forest
31374 US Highway 2
Libby, MT 59923-3022
(406) 293-6211

# Montana Waterfalls Western Region

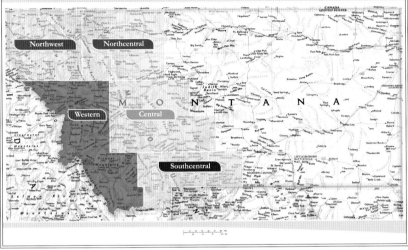

# Abha Falls

## DESCRIPTION

If you have made it to the first set of steep switchbacks after about 2 miles up Bass Creek, then you're virtually at Abha Falls, you just didn't realize it. If you listen closely, you can hear the creek's excited roar to the south. This hidden wonder bounces down a few slides, over a shelf and down 40 feet into a misty chasm. If you're not satisfied with the view from the top, a quick bushwhack to the bottom will give you a view very few may have seen.

*Abha Falls*

## SUMMARY

| | |
|---|---|
| **Stream**<br>• Bass Creek | **Watershed**<br>• Bitterroot River |
| **Size**<br>• Creek | **Forest**<br>• Bitterroot National Forest |
| **Height**<br>• 40 ft. | **Hike**<br>• 6 mi. - Moderate hike |
| **Formation**<br>• Terraced | **Road access**<br>• Easy highway/road access |
| **Elevation**<br>• 4800 | **Season**<br>• Spring, Summer, Fall |
| **Area**<br>• Western | **Latitude**<br>• 46.580362 |
| **County**<br>• Ravalli | **Longitude**<br>• -114.204004 |

## ACCESS

From Missoula drive 13 miles South on US-93. When you get to Bass Creek Road, hang a right. Stay on this road until it becomes Charles Waters Camp Road. After you cross the bridge over Bass Creek, continue on Larry Creek Loop until you reach the trail head. From here hike about 3 miles up Bass Creek until you come to the first switchback that is within earshot of the creek. You will know you are near the falls when the trail really starts to climb and bedrock appears. At the switchback, head southeast down to the creek and follow the sound to the falls. The falls will be an obvious drop into a narrow chasm. There are a few more nice waterfalls upstream including one, Indie Falls, which has a sheer drop that is very beautiful. To get to these waterfalls, go back to the trail and keep heading up the creek. You will notice the falls on your left.

## HISTORY

In July 1877, the Nez Percé Indians were driven from their homeland in the Clearwater Valley in Idaho. After a fatiguing fight in the Battle of the Clearwater, they attempted to make a break for the Bitterroot Valley in Montana to the east. Captain Rawn and some Missoula volunteers were notified of their approach and quickly erected a wooden barricade in an attempt to stop the anticipated advance of the tribe and its leader, Chief Joseph. However, the plan fell apart when

the Nez Percé slipped up a steep ravine and bypassed the entire racket. The failure of the barricade earned it the nickname, "Fort Fizzle." From here the Nez Percé traveled south, passing Bass Creek, and continued to the Big Hole Valley where the Battle of the Big Hole ensued.

## GEOLOGY

The Bitterroot Mountains and Bass Creek are located on the eastern edge of the Idaho Batholith. Geological evidence shows that at one point around

*Unnamed Falls up Bass Creek*

80 million years ago, a giant mass of granitic magma pushed itself up in a bulging fashion. The overlying host rock began to facture and slide off to the east, creating a metamorphic zone known as Mylonite. Similar to ice skates gliding across ice, the friction between the two created heat that melted and deformed the rock. This process acted as a lubricant, enabling the fracture zone and

its overlying rock to slide off like a gargantuan deck of cards. The friction left linear stretch marks in the rock that angle down to the east at a gentle 30-degree slope. The further you hike up many of the western Bitterroot creeks, the less these stretch marks are noticeable.

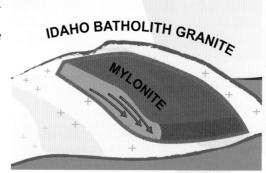

IDAHO BATHOLITH GRANITE

MYLONITE

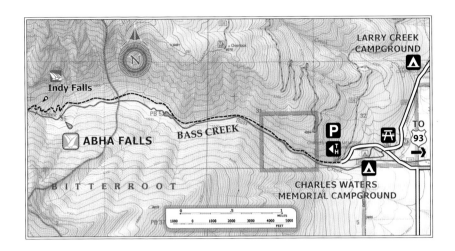

## CAMPING

**Charles Waters Memorial Campground** (USFS) is up Bass Creek Road 2.1 miles from US-93, 4 miles south of Florence. The campground is located just inside the Bitterroot National Forest boundary and has 28 campsites, potable water, and wheelchair-accessible restrooms for a $10 per day fee. Charles Waters Memorial Campground is open April 1 through Nov. 1.

**Larry Creek Group Site Campground** (USFS) has two group tent campsites. The campground also has potable water and handicapped-accessible restrooms. The fee is $30.00 per night per group

**Bitterroot National Forest**
1801 North First Street
Hamilton, MT 59840
406-363-7100

# Brave Bear Falls

## DESCRIPTION

This is one of those exceptional spots within the vast array of Bitterroot Valley tributaries where unbroken granite bedrock refuses to give way and cradles a myriad of slides, cascades and small waterfalls. Watch for a 7-foot falls followed by several cascades next to a cliff and a stunning view. Farther up the valley are three off-the-path gems that are well worth the bushwhacking. Ammons Falls can be heard from the trail and is just downstream from where the trail crosses the creek. Fallen Pyramid can be accessed by leaving the trail just before the crossing, by staying on the south side of the creek and bushwhacking upstream for a quarter-mile. Fallen Pyramid is a picturesque sheer falls dropping onto a triangular boulder. The large and more spectacular Jess Adam Falls drops a sheer 30 feet. To get to this one, follow the trail as it crosses both the main and north forks, then for another quarter-mile. When you start hearing a loud roar, bushwhack down to the south fork of Bear Creek and locate the growling. Hopefully, it won't be a bear.

*Brave Bear Falls*

## SUMMARY

| | |
|---|---|
| **Stream**<br>• Bear Creek | **Watershed**<br>• Bitterroot River |
| **Size**<br>• Creek | **Forest**<br>• Bitterroot National Forest |
| **Height**<br>• 49 ft. | **Hike**<br>• 3 mi. - Easy hike |
| **Formation**<br>• Cascade | **Road access**<br>• Dirt roads |
| **Elevation**<br>• 3855 | **Season**<br>• Spring, Summer and Fall |
| **Area**<br>• Western | **Latitude**<br>• 46.382013 |
| **County**<br>• Ravalli | **Longitude**<br>• -114.278338 |

## ACCESS

From Victor, head west out of town on Pleasant View Drive for 2.3 miles to Red Crow Road. Turn left at Red Crow Road and travel 1.1 miles to Bear Creek Road. Turn right onto Bear Creek Road for 2.8 miles to the end of the road and the trailhead for Bear Creek Trail (TR 5).

*At the foothills, bluebells and a bitterroot flower*

## HISTORY

The Bitterroot Valley is named after the bitterroot (Lewisia rediviva) plant, which was an important wild crop harvested by numerous Native American tribes of the western United States. Families would gather the root before the flower bloomed by digging it up, and prepare the roots by boiling, steaming or pit-roasting them. The natives thought this was a treat, whereas the pioneers thought it was bitter—hence the common name. The bitterroot is also the state flower of Montana. It was named by Captain Meriwether Lewis, who collected the flowers on his return trip in 1806 while traveling through the Bitterroot Valley.

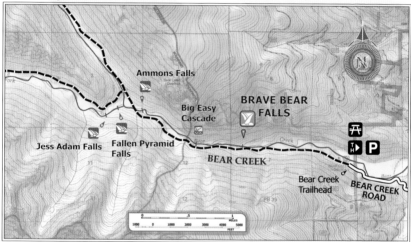

## CAMPING

**Charles Waters Memorial campground** (U.S. Forest Service) is up Bass Creek Road 2.1 miles from US-93, 4 miles south of Florence. Located just inside the Bitterroot National Forest boundary, the campground has 28 sites, potable water, and wheelchair-accessible restrooms, with a $10 per day fee. Charles Waters Memorial campground is open from April 1 until November 1.

**Blodgett Creek Campground** (U.S. Forest Service), 4.1 miles from Hamilton, is a small pack in–pack out campground. There are seven sites available and the campground is equipped with restrooms.

Bitterroot National Forest
1801 North First Street
Hamilton, MT 59840
406-363-7100

# Como Falls

## DESCRIPTION

What a remarkable day hike this one is. A lake, towering granite spires, large angular boulders and glistening waterfalls will greet you.

To get to the falls, take Como Loop National Recreational Trail. It starts at the southwest end of the Upper Como Lake Campground. As the trail winds among towering ponderosa pines just off the north shore of Como Lake, you can't help but notice the incredible scenic beauty of the lake and the Bitterroot Mountains. At places the trail becomes a little cliffed-out, but it really is a nice 2.3-mile trail to the falls that even a family could enjoy.

The falls are simply a series of cascades along Rock Creek which empties into Como Lake. (The falls are also known as Rock Creek Falls.) Farther up the trail, going west along Rock Creek is Two Brothers Falls. Seen from a distance, the creek splits in two around a wide, rock-faced island. Another ¼ mile up the trail and then a bushwhack to the creek will bring you to the ledges along the north side of the creek. This is an excellent place to picnic or camp. Swimming in the small pools between the bedrock drops is always a pleasant way to spend the afternoon.

*Como Falls, also known as Rock Creek Falls*

| Stream | Watershed |
|---|---|
| • Rock Creek | • Bitterroot River |
| **Size** | **Forest** |
| • Creek | • Bitterroot National Forest |
| **Height** | **Hike** |
| • 20 ft. | • 4.6 mi. - Moderate hike |
| **Formation** | **Road access** |
| • Slide | • Easy highway/road access |
| **Elevation** | **Season** |
| • 4268 | • Spring, Summer and Fall |
| **Area** | **Latitude** |
| • Northwest | • 46.047263 |
| **County** | **Longitude** |
| • Ravalli | • -114.296951 |

## ACCESS

From Darby, drive north on US-93 for 4.1 miles to Lake Como Road. Keep right and stay on Como Lake Road for another 0.7 miles, then turn left into the Como Lake campgrounds (upper and lower). Stay to the right (north side of the lake), heading toward the upper campground, and keep going until you reach the end of the road and the trailhead.

*Northern leopard frog*

## HISTORY

The Nez Perce (Nee-Me-Poo) National Historic Trail was designated by Congress in 1986, under the National Trails System Act of 1968, which allowed for recreational, scenic and historical trails nationwide. This trail follows the path taken by 750 Nez Perce Indian men, women and children, led by Chief Joseph and others, when they were being pursued by the United States Army. The trail starts from the homeland of the Nez Perce near Wallowa Lake, Oregon, and ends south of Chinook, Montana, in the Bear Paw Mountains. The historic trail is marked along the route by the many skirmishes and battles for over 1,170 miles. When the Nez Perce were forced in a peaceful move to Lapwai Indian Reservation, the tribe's chiefs (Looking Glass, Ollokot, Joseph, White Bird, among others) decided their last hope for peace was to go to Canada. Their circuitous route (part of it in the Bitterroot Valley) is now known as the Nez Perce National Trail.

*Two Brothers Falls*

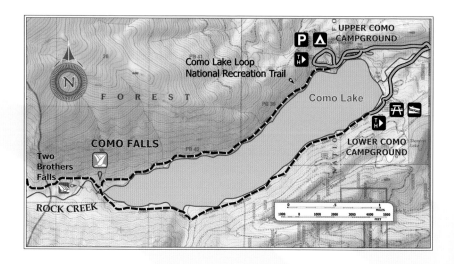

## CAMPING

**Lower Como Campground** (United States Forest Service) is situated off of the alluring Lake Como (elevation 4,500 feet). There are 11 campsites available from May 15 to Sept. 30. The campground has handicapped-accessible toilets, potable water and trash pickup. Recreational opportunities include fishing, swimming, boating and hiking.

**Upper Como Campground** (United States Forest Service) on the upper end of Lake Como has 11 campsites available year-around. It has handicapped-accessible toilets, potable water and trash pickup.

Bitterroot National Forest
1801 North First Street
Hamilton, MT 59840
406-363-7100

## DESCRIPTION

This is a fantastic destination for those willing to put up with a little undeveloped access, and will remain a vivid memory. The waterfall spouts twenty feet into a deep green semi-round pool. Nearby is a grove of old-growth cedar trees. One, near the road and just upstream of the falls, measures nearly eight feet in diameter at its base. It's amazing that these trees were left untouched by logging. Trees like this are a treasure to all of us and serve a purpose far beyond their economic value. Below the falls is a series of cascades. All of them are well worth the bushwhack to witness them, especially the last, Geometry Falls. Its large angular overhanging cave is stunning.

From the shot-up road sign that vaguely says "250" , hike the overgrown old logging road southwest for a mile. The falls is on the left and to the south just off the road and is the only obvious falls viewable from the road. If you have time during the day, a bit farther up the road is the access point to the South Fork of Trout Creek and Heart Lake. A mere half mile up Trail 171 brings you to a smaller set of pristine water features generally know as the South Fork Cascades.

*Emerald Sun Falls*

SUMMARY

| Stream | Watershed |
|---|---|
| • North Fork Trout Creek | • Clark Fork |
| **Size** | **Forest** |
| • Creek | • Lolo National Forest |
| **Height** | **Hike** |
| • 20 ft. | • 2 mi. - Easy hike |
| **Formation** | **Road access** |
| • Punchbowl | • Dirt roads |
| **Elevation** | **Season** |
| • 4560 | • Spring, Summer and Fall |
| **Area** | **Latitude** |
| • Western | • 47.002694 |
| **County** | **Longitude** |
| • Mineral | • -115.001514 |

### ACCESS

From Superior, west of Interstate 90, head southeast on Diamond Road for 6.5 miles to Trout Creek Road. Merge onto Trout Creek Road, driving some 11.7 miles up to a partially blasted sign reading 250 and to where a side road comes in from the right (North West). Park here. You have gone too far by 1/2 mile if your come to where the main road crosses the creek. To get the to the access point for the South Fork of Trout Creek Cascades, keep going one the main road for two more miles to the trailhead (TR 171). This is just before the road crosses the South Fork of Trout Creek.

*Geometry Falls*

## HISTORY

The Mullan Road is a 624-mile-long road stretching from Walla Walla, Washington to Fort Benton, Montana. It was named after Captain John Mullan, who was in charge of the construction crew that built the wagon road through the Rocky Mountains. This was a difficult feat over the remote Rockies; there weren't even trails along the route. Built between 1859 to 1861, the road was the first built in the western United States using engineering principles. Portions of the Mullan Road can be seen today along I-90 in western Montana.

This area was also very rich in placer gold. Cedar Creek, one drainage northwest from the falls, briefly produced so much gold that the region's newspaper was originally named *Missoula and Cedar Creek Pioneer*. It continues today as the *Missoulian*.

*Western red cedar*

## CAMPING

**Trout Creek Campground** (USFS) is around 7 miles southwest of Superior on the Trout Creek Road. There are 12 forested campsites available with some of the campsites along the creek side. There are vault toilets, potable water and garbage service from Memorial Day weekend through Labor Day weekend. Fees are $6 per night and an additional-vehicle fee of $3 per night. Activities include fishing (access to Trout Creek), hiking, picnicking and bird watching.

**Quartz Flat Campground** (USFS) is 11 miles east of Superior just off of Interstate 90. This campground is within walking distance of the Clark Fork River. It has 77 campsites, there are both flush and vault toilets, has potable water available and there is a RV waste disposal site ($2 fee if not staying in campground). The campground fee is $10 per night with an additional-vehicle fee of $5 per night. River access and a self-guided nature trail add to this woodsy recreation site.

Lolo National Forest
Fort Missoula Bldg. 24
Missoula, MT 59804
406-329-3750

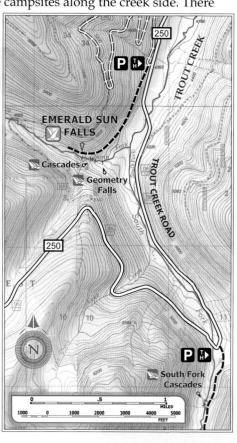

## DESCRIPTION

At the start of the trail you are right next to shimmering Glacier Creek and for the next 1.5 miles you're either next to the creek or not far from it as you walk up to Glacier Lake. This beautiful hike into the Mission Mountain Wilderness is fairly easy but gets a little harder as you near the lake. Once on the shoreline, you will immediately gaze upon Glacier Creek Falls as it careens down a shelf of rock. A few kayakers report bushwhacking up to the falls in search of kayakable whitewater above. Instead, they ran into a wolverine, nervously clicking its claws on a log across the creek. The surrounding area truly expresses itself in the form of pure wilderness.

*Glacier Creek Falls*

| Stream | Watershed |
|---|---|
| • Glacier Creek | • Swan River |
| **Size** | **Forest** |
| • Creek | • Flathead National Forest |
| **Height** | **Hike** |
| • 130 ft. | • 3 mi. - Moderate hike |
| **Formation** | **Road access** |
| • Cascade | • Dirt roads |
| **Elevation** | **Season** |
| • 5404 | • Summer |
| **Area** | **Latitude** |
| • Western | • 47.367374 |
| **County** | **Longitude** |
| • Missoula | • -113.833122 |

## ACCESS

From Condon, travel south on Montana Highway 83 for 5.0 miles to Kraft Creek Road (FR 561). Turn right at FR 561 winding into the incredible Mission Mountains 13.5 miles to the trailhead of Glacier Creek Trail. There is a large parking area with a restroom at the beginning of this TR 708.

*Mission Mountains looking west*

## HISTORY

The Mission Mountain Wilderness totals some 73,877 acres of pristine, scenic beauty. Congress designated this as a Wilderness Area in 1975. Its idyllic beauty is home to a dozen or more mountain peaks over 9,000 feet, where permanent alpine snow fields melting create hundreds of small glacier-formed lakes called tarns. Located in the Flathead National Forest, it makes up most of the eastern half of the Mission Mountain Range, while most of the western half of the range is Confederated Salish and Kootenai Tribal Wilderness Area.

*Glacier Lake*

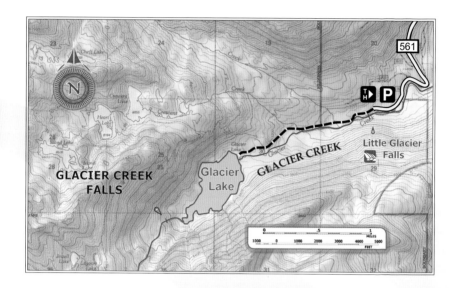

## CAMPING

**Lindbergh Lake Campground** (USFS elevation 4,367') is a pack in–pack out campground. There are 22 campsites available, wheelchair accessible restrooms, fishing access and boat ramp. The vista of the lake and the Mission Mountains is special.

**Holland Lake Campground** (USFS), located right on beautiful Holland Lake, has two loops. First is Larch Loop, which is on a small bluff overlooking the lake. The second loop, a little more than three fourth of the way down Holland Lake Road, is called Bay Loop. This campground is situated around a gorgeous little bay. Combined there are 39 camping units, drinking water, trash pickup, toilet facilities and a $12/day fee with two weeks maximum stay. This is grizzly bear country — you must know and practice safe food storage techniques.

Flathead National Forest
650 Wolfpack Way
Kalispell, MT 59901
406-758-5200

## DESCRIPTION

Salish-Kootenai tribal land is where the mysterious Grey Wolf Falls is located. It is the last and largest in a series of cascades and waterfalls at the end of the road. From the parking area, walk back down the road about 50 yards, then head to the right through the forest toward the cascade. If you come to a falls that plunges directly into a deep round pool, then you are at Jocko falls.

Grey Wolf is the next drop right after the pool. It is a magnificent double leap onto a triangular boulder within the depths of a narrow chasm. Mountainous views can be seen from here as well as panoramic perspectives of the creek. Be extra careful around the south side of this falls, because it is extremely steep and the cliffs drop off sharply.

*Jocko Falls*

SUMMARY

| Stream | Watershed |
|---|---|
| • North Fork Jocko River | • Flathead River |
| **Size** | **Forest** |
| • Creek | • Confederated Salish and Kootenai Tribes |
| **Height** | **Hike** |
| • 23 ft. | • 0.1 mi. - short walk from road |
| **Formation** | **Road access** |
| • Punchbowl | • Rough roads at times |
| **Elevation** | **Season** |
| • 4446 | • Summer and Fall |
| **Area** | **Latitude** |
| • Western | • 47.232508 |
| **County** | **Longitude** |
| • Lake | • -113.802352 |

From St. Ignatius head southeast on St. Mary's Road–Jocko Lakes Road (BIA 1012) for 14.4 miles to Jocko Canyon Road (BIA 146). Turn left on BIA 146 for 3.1 miles to North Fork Jocko access road. Turn left on North Fork access road 1.4 miles to a small parking area for the falls.

*National Bison Range and Mission Mountains*

# HISTORY

St. Ignatius Mission was established in 1854 and built by Native Americans under the guidance of Roman Catholic missionaries. There are 58 original murals by Brother Joseph Carignano on the mission's walls and ceiling.

The National Bison Range at Moiese is home to some 500 bison (or, buffalo as Montanans call them). The Red Sleep Mountain Drive is a year-around self-guided auto tour, where visitors with sharp eyes spot elk, deer, antelope, and Rocky Mountain sheep as well as bison.

*Grey Wolf Falls*

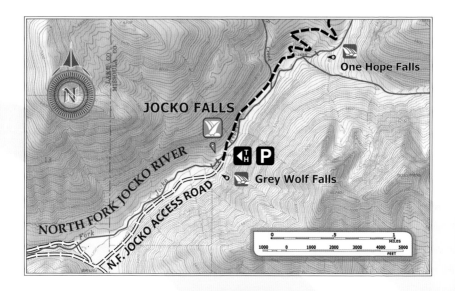

## CAMPING

**North Fork Jocko Campground** (CSKT) has only 1 campsite. There is a restroom, and the site has fishing access. Note: These are Confederated Salish and Kootenai Tribal campgrounds. You will need a CSKT conservation license and a camping stamp.

**Twin Lake Campground** (CSKT, elevation 4147') has 11 campsites available. The campground has restrooms, and there is a boat launch accessing Twin Lake.

Confederated Salish & Kootenai Tribes
42487 Complex Blvd.
P.O. Box 278
Pablo, MT 59855
406-675-2700

## DESCRIPTION

This is a very beautiful, unusual, triple-tiered waterfall, hidden in a narrow but deep mini-gorge. After a short walk along an old logging road, you begin to hear the creek roar as it drops over cascades. Along this road you will see evidence of ancient, fossilized, Precambrian rock from a sea bottom one million years old that is imprinted with water ripples. As you start the hike to the falls by walking past the gated Forest Service Road and head south for a distance of about a 0.25 mile, you will see evidence of some ancient fossilized Precambrian sea-bottom mud.

*Lodgepole Creek Falls*

SUMMARY

| Stream | Watershed |
|---|---|
| • Lodgepole Creek | • Blackfoot River |
| **Size** | **Forest** |
| • Creek | • Lolo National Forest |
| **Height** | **Hike** |
| • 75 ft. | • 0.5 mi. - short walk from road |
| **Formation** | **Road access** |
| • Tiered | • Rough roads at times |
| **Elevation** | **Season** |
| • 5138 | • Summer and Fall |
| **Area** | **Latitude** |
| • Western | • 47.206275 |
| **County** | **Longitude** |
| • Powell | • -113.200979 |

## ACCESS

From MH 200, take the Ovando turnoff and drive north on Forest Service Road 107 (Monture Creek Road) for 7 miles to Cottonwood Lakes Road. Turn left on Cottonwood Lakes Road for 1.0 mile to Dunham Creek Road (FR 131). Turn right, following this road up Lodgepole Creek for 7.3 miles. After crossing over the creek the second time, you will find a locked gate for FS Road 4397. Start your hike to the falls by walking around the gate down the road for a distance of about a quarter of a mile, heading south. When the creek takes a 90-degree turn to the right (heading west), walk down to the falls. Be sure to stay away from the cliffs on the eastern bank. It's a steep bushwhack to the falls but well worth it.

*Water rippled pre-cambrian mudstone near falls*

## HISTORY

Indians, frontiersmen and explorers historically used many of the routes in their travels through today's Bob Marshall Wilderness Complex. The Bob Marshall Wilderness, the Great Bear Wilderness and the Scapegoat Wilderness collectively form the complex. This was all started in 1964, when Congress passed the first Wilderness Act. The complex now spans an area of over 1.5 million acres. It has some 450-plus maintained trails totaling well over a 1,000 miles in the area. The BMWC is managed by four national forest: Flathead, Helena, Lewis and Clark and Lolo; and five Forest Service Ranger Districts: Spotted Bear, Hungry Horse, Lincoln, Rocky Mountain and Seeley Lake. BMWC is also listed on the National Register of Historic Places.

*Dunham Falls*

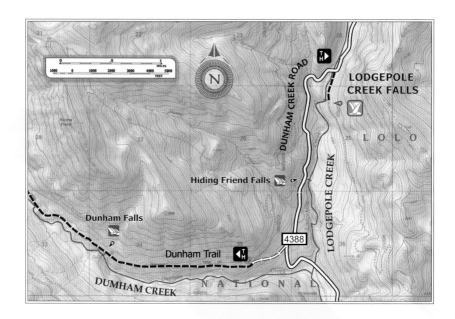

## CAMPING

**Monture Creek Campground** (USFS), which offers no-fee camping, is 7.5 miles north of MH 200 and the MontureRoad (RS Road 107) junction. This campground, at 4,100' elevation, is located alongside Monture Creek and is available from June 1 to October 30. There are 5 campsites and toilet facilities, but no drinking water. The trailhead for TR 25 is adjacent to Monture Creek Campground and offers horse corrals. Other trails branch out for access into Bob Marshall Wilderness and the Scapegoat Wilderness areas.

Lolo National Forest Supervisor's Office
Fort Missoula Bldg. 24
Missoula MT 59804
406-329-3750

# Lost Creek Falls

## DESCRIPTION

A great interpretive sign is at the trailhead to Lost Creek Falls. The trail is a paved, medium handicapped-difficulty, hike to the falls. Benches are along this forested trail to sit, rest and take in nature's beauty, that being something all ages can enjoy. Lost Creek State Park is in the Flint Creek Range in the Beaverhead–Deerlodge National Forest.

*Lost Creek Falls*

SUMMARY

| Stream | Watershed |
|---|---|
| • Lost Creek | • Clark Fork |
| **Size** | **Forest** |
| • Creek | • Beaverhead-Deerlodge |
| **Height** | **Hike** |
| • 35 ft. | • .25 mi. - short walk from road |
| **Formation** | **Road access** |
| • Terraced | • Dirt roads |
| **Elevation** | **Season** |
| • 6831 | • Spring, Summer and Fall |
| **Area** | **Latitude** |
| • Western | • 46.223226 |
| **County** | **Longitude** |
| • Deer Lodge | • -113.039746 |

### ACCESS

From Anaconda, take Montana Highway 1 east 3.8 miles to Montana Secondary 48. Turn left on Montana Secondary 48 for only 0.3 miles to Montana Secondary 273. Turn left onto Galen Road (MH 273) for 1.9 miles. Turn left at Lost Creek Road, driving 9.1 miles through Lost Creek State Park and the trailhead at the northwest end of the park.

*Mountain locoweed*

## HISTORY

The area surrounding Lost Creek has a colorful mining history. The Cable Mine, to its southwest, reportedly produced a gold nugget that rivaled even the largest ever found. Also near here is the ghost town of Southern Cross. From the 1880s to the 1940s, it was the site of a vibrant gold mining community.

*Lost Creek State Park*

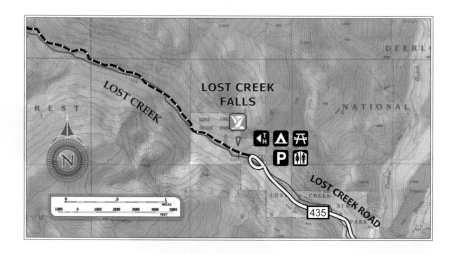

## CAMPING

**Lost Creek State Park** (FWP) is a narrow, boulder-strewn, forested canyon with spectacular grey limestone cliffs and towering 1200' granite formations rising from the valley floor. The 1993, the state legislature designated Lost Creek as a 502.5-acre Primitive State Park, with a pack in–pack out trash policy. There are 10 campsites, drinking water (hand pumped), handicapped accessible toilets, and $7/day fee with a 7-day limit. This park, located in the Beaverhead–Deerlodge National Forest, is very well maintained by the Department of the Montana Fish, Game, Wildlife and Parks.

Montana Fish, Wildlife & Parks
Parks Division
406-444-3750

**Racetrack Campground and Picnic Area** (USFS) is a pack in–pack out campground 11 miles west from the Racetrack exit (exit 195) off Interstate 90. There are 13 camping units, potable water and handicapped accessible vault toilets. This campground also has a picnic area and access to roaring Racetrack Creek. Camping is limited to 16 days and there is no fee.

Pintler Ranger District
406-859-3211

## DESCRIPTION

Humans in kayaks learn to fly here. When the water is high, Lower Boulder Falls creates a ski jump, sliding down and blasting over a curved lip in the rock. The total drop is only around 20 feet, but awesome nonetheless. From the trailhead, it's an easy quarter-mile hike to the falls. When the trail makes its first switch back turn, leave the trail and follow the path to the creek and falls. Farther up the creek you will find more water slides and cascades. If you're feeling really ambitious and need more of a hike, head up the trail another 3 miles to Upper Boulder Creek Falls. It's much larger and more dramatic but a bit dangerous at the edge, since the slick bedrock slopes down into the waterfall. A misstep here would provide a slip-and-slide ride only your friends would remember.

*Lower Boulder Creek Falls*

SUMMARY

| Stream | Watershed |
|---|---|
| • *Boulder Creek* | • *Bitterroot River* |
| **Size** | **Forest** |
| • *Creek* | • *Bitterroot National Forest* |
| **Height** | **Hike** |
| • *23 ft.* | • *1 mi. - Easy hike* |
| **Formation** | **Road access** |
| • *Slide* | • *Dirt roads* |
| **Elevation** | **Season** |
| • *4678* | • *All* |
| **Area** | **Latitude** |
| • *Western* | • *45.832068* |
| **County** | **Longitude** |
| • *Ravalli* | • *-114.262018* |

### ACCESS

From Darby, drive south on US 93 for 7.4 miles to the Connor Cut-off/Forgotten Lane road. Turn right onto the Connor Cutoff Road and drive 1.2 miles to the West Fork Road/Montana Secondary 493. Turn left onto the West Fork road and drive 10.1 miles to Sam Billings Road/FR 5731. Turn right on FR 5731, traveling 0.8 miles then continuing up Boulder Creek Road another 0.4 mile to the trailhead.

*Trapper Peak*

## HISTORY

The trailhead to Boulder Creek passes the Sam Billings Campground, named to honor the forester who saw that the big pines here should be left for people to enjoy.

While hiking up the creek drainage, keep an eye out for large ponderosa pine trees that may have large, wide scars on their trunks. This is a result of Native Americans peeling off the tree's bark to access the tree's sweet cambium layer. If you look closely at the base of the scar, sometimes you can see the small hatch marks of a stone tool. This practice did not kill the tree, and now these trees are living testaments to the people who once lived in the area. Archaeologists utilizing tree-ring dating found that some of these trees were scarred more than 300 years ago.

Historic trail-blazes are also evident on the large trees along the Boulder Creek Trail. Sometimes these marks were called "candle" blazes (to light your way through the forest) because they are a short cut (the flame) above a longer vertical cut (the candle).

## CAMPING

**Sam Billings Memorial Campground** is adjacent to Boulder Creek a mile up from the confluence with the West Fork of the Bitterroot River. This is a Pack-In, Pack Out campground with 30 RV sites and 12 tent campsites. There are vault restrooms and there is fishing access to Boulder Creek. Fee: None

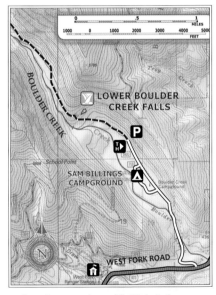

**Rombo Campground** is just off of the west Fork of the Bitterroot River. There are 30 RV sites with 15 tent campsites, there is potable water, vault restrooms and it has a campground host. It is only open during the summer. There is access to the river and an $8.00/night camping fee.

BITTERROOT NATIONAL FOREST
1801 North First Street
Hamilton, MT 59840
406-363-7100

## DESCRIPTION

Surrounded by Kakashe Mountain (8,575'), Mountaineer Peak (9,261') and Lowary Peak (9,369') the Mission Creek Valley offers an absolutely breathtaking view. The canyon walls are so steep they give the illusion of being in the Himalayas.

The Mission Falls Trail, going into the unbelievable Mission Mountains, gradually climbs up about 50 feet, then you can fork off to the right to view Lower Mission Falls. For what this cascade lacks in vertical drop, it makes up in its unique display of aquatic dynamics. Water rushes down a steep ramp before splitting around layered bedrock. The left channel hurdles over an uneven vertical drop while the right channel funnels down another ramp to meet the left channel again at the base of the falls. This, in combination with the moss and cedar atmosphere, make for some excellent photography and a relaxing experience.

As you continue to walk up the Mission Falls Trail, the hiking difficulty increases immediately. This is standard fare for hiking on the trails in the west side of the Mission Mountains. On the tribal side the trails tend to be rough and steep, with a lot of switchbacks. From Lower Mission Falls, elevation 3,619', you hike up 2.5 miles and 1,260' in elevation to reach awesome Mission Falls cascading down nearly 1,000'. The trail continuing up after Mission Falls is called the Lucifer Lake Trail. Hiking another mile up and 980' in elevation gain you will then reach the totally spectacular Elizabeth Falls. Be very careful hiking to the edges of Elizabeth and Mission Falls. Their edges are both slippery and sloping.

*Mission Falls*

## SUMMARY

| | |
|---|---|
| **Stream**<br>• Mission Creek | **Watershed**<br>• Flathead River |
| **Size**<br>• Creek | **Forest**<br>• Confederated Salish & Kootenai Tribes |
| **Height**<br>• 975 ft. | **Hike**<br>• 3.75 mi. - Difficult hike |
| **Formation**<br>• Shoestring | **Road access**<br>• Rough roads at times |
| **Elevation**<br>• 5955 | **Season**<br>• Spring, Summer and Fall |
| **Area**<br>• Western | **Latitude**<br>• 47.339928 |
| **County**<br>• Lake | **Longitude**<br>• -113.928695 |

## ACCESS

From St. Ignatius, drive south on St. Marys Lake Road for 0.4 mile to Mission Dam Road. Turn left onto Mission Dam Road, driving along the north side of scenic Mission Reservoir, 5.9 miles to the trailhead at the end of the road. Note that this waterfall is on tribal land, and you will need a Confederated Salish and Kootenai Tribal conservation license to hike on tribal land. These generally inexpensive permits can be purchased at most outdoor recreation stores in Missoula, Polson or Ronan.

*American bison*

## HISTORY

The Mission Mountains Tribal Wilderness Area covers almost 92,000 acres in the Flathead National Forest. Its mountain peaks range from around 4,000' in the foothills, to 10,000'. The historic tribal wilderness management plan was formed in 1982 and was the first time that Indian tribes determined on their own to protect a significant portion of their land as wilderness. Glaciers carving the valleys created more than 112 lakes in this area.

The St. Ignatius Mission in the nearby town of St. Ignatius is another point of interest. Built in the early 1890s, it is famous for the 61 original fresco paintings by Brother Joseph Carignano, S.J., covering its walls and ceilings. The building is listed on the National Register of Historic Places.

The National Bison Range at Moiese was established 1908 to help conserve and support the great American bison. Administered by the U.S. Fish and Wildlife Service, this 100-acre range is one of the oldest wildlife refuges in the United States. There are over 500 buffalo (as they are known locally) roaming the reserve, and this is also where the deer and antelope play, along with elk and bighorn sheep, and numerous species of birds.

*Lower Mission Falls*

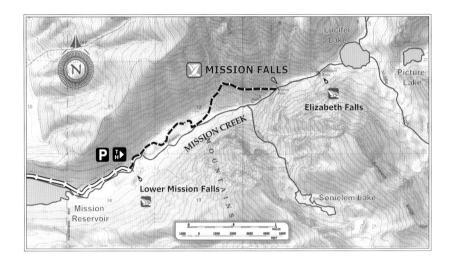

## CAMPING

**Mission Dam Campground** is on Confederated Salish–Kootenai Tribal land. To camp there requires you to purchase their conservation license for $11/season (runs from March to end of February), and purchase a $10/season camping permit. This primitive campground has a restroom, picnic tables, some grated fire-pots and the most unbelievable view of Mission Lake and the Mission Mountains.

*Mission Lake and the Mission Mountains*

# Morrell Falls

## DESCRIPTION

The Morrell Falls National Historic Trail is a 2.3-mile hike into the Lolo National Forest. This is a fairly easy day hike that really doesn't have any steep grades to it. The trail leads through tightly spaced stands of lodgepole pine, past the 23-acre Morrell Lake and on to a series of waterfalls. Towards the end of the trail you wind around a marsh, and then you hear the falls. Just past an old-growth-timber stand, the view opens onto a small clearing and 90′ Morrell Falls.

*Morrell Falls*

| | |
|---|---|
| **Stream**<br>• Morell Creek | **Watershed**<br>• Blackfoot River |
| **Size**<br>• Creek | **Forest**<br>• Lolo National Forest |
| **Height**<br>• 90 ft. | **Hike**<br>• 3.1 mi. - Moderate hike |
| **Formation**<br>• Horsetail | **Road access**<br>• Dirt roads |
| **Elevation**<br>• 5121 | **Season**<br>• Winter |
| **Area**<br>• Western | **Latitude**<br>• 47.300973 |
| **County**<br>• Missoula | **Longitude**<br>• -113.462892 |

## ACCESS

From Seely Lake drive north 0.25 miles to Cottonwood Lakes Road (FR 447). Take the first left at the fork then go 2.0 miles to West Morrell Road (FR 467). Turn north for 7 miles to Pyramid Pass Road. Drive only 0.25 mile north to Morrell Falls Road (FR 4369). Turn north again one mile to the trailhead.

*Small mountain lake off the west side of the road*

## HISTORY

Seely Lake is one part of the Clearwater Chain-of-Lakes. There are 24 or more lakes in the Clearwater River Valley. These lakes — which include Salmon Lake, Seely Lake, Lake Inez, Lake Alva and Rainy Lake — are easily accessed via Montana State Highway 83, and most have developed campgrounds nearby. From its headwaters in the Swan Range in Lolo National Forest, the Clearwater River flows south to its confluence with the Blackfoot River near the junction of MH 83 and MH 200.

*Creekside moss*

CAMPING

**Big Larch Campground** (USFS; elev. 4,000') is one mile north of the town of Seely Lake on Montana State Highway 83. Right off beautiful Seely Lake, the 50 campsites and 8 picnic sites are nestled among towering ponderosa pines, with an awesome view of the Mission Mountains. There is a $10/day fee for individual campsites and a $35/day for group campsites. Potable water is available, and there are handicapped accessible toilets, a concrete boat launch, boat trailer parking and an on-site campground host.

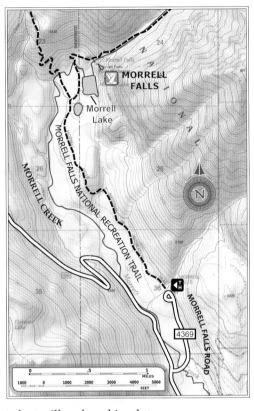

At the trailhead for Morrell Falls there are toilets, but no potable water. Overnight camping is permitted at the trailhead parking lot.

*Don't worry about the bears, watch out for these guys (author Nathan Johnson)*

Lolo National Forest
Fort Missoula Bldg. 24
Missoula, MT 59804
406-329-3750

# Pintler Falls

## DESCRIPTION

Like an island, the bedrock cradling Pintler Falls rises like a whale from the deep. An idyllic meadow precedes the falls and, after some refreshing rapids, Pintler Creek meanders into Pinter Lake. The falls makes up for its lack of height in its sheer beauty, a crystal-clear cascade rumbling over the granite roots of the Pintler Mountains, surrounded by a thick forest. Pintler Creek flows into the scenic and pristine Pintler Lake.

*Pintler Falls in May*

| Stream | Watershed |
|---|---|
| • *Pintler Creek* | • *Jefferson River* |
| **Size** | **Forest** |
| • *Creek* | • *Beaverhead-Deerlodge* |
| **Height** | **Hike** |
| • *30 ft.* | • *0.5 mi. - Easy hike* |
| **Formation** | **Road access** |
| • *Cascade* | • *Dirt roads* |
| **Elevation** | **Season** |
| • *6434* | • *Spring, Summer and Fall* |
| **Area** | **Latitude** |
| • *Western* | • *46.410212* |
| **County** | **Longitude** |
| • *Deerlodge* | • *112.963142* |

## ACCESS

From Wisdom, head northeast on Montana Highway 43 for about 15 miles. Take a left at N Fork Road and follow this for 5 miles. Take a right on FSR 185, driving past Pintler Lake and ending at the Pintler Falls trailhead.

*Trumpeter swans on upper Madison River*

## HISTORY

The Big Hole Battlefied is just west of Wisdom, Montana. Here an epic battle took place between the fleeing Nez Pierce Indians (see Snowshoe Falls entry) and the U.S. Army in 1877.

## CAMPING

**Pintler Campground and Picnic Area** (USFS) is a really small, unique pack in-pack out campground. There are only 2 campsites, but potable water is available along with a vaulted toilet. This beautiful little campground has access to Pintler Creek and is next to Pintler Lake. No fee.

Beaverhead–Deerlodge National Forest
420 Barrett Street
Dillon, MT 59725-3572
406-683-3900

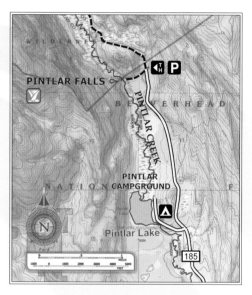

**Dickie Bridge Campground** (BLM) is 18 miles west of Divide, next to the Big Hole River. There are 8 campsites, vault toilets, boat launch and a 14-day stay limit. Fee is $8.00/night.

Bureau Of Land Management
106 North Parkmont
Butte, MT 59701
406-533-7600

*Pintler Lake at Pintler Campground*

## DESCRIPTION

Nestled at the head of Rock Creek Lake shimmers Rock Creek Falls — multi-tiered and rumbling through a jagged gorge and into the lake. The falls is the largest and topmost of the many cascades and slides that make up a quarter mile of falling water along Rock Creek.

*Rock Creek Falls*

SUMMARY

| | |
|---|---|
| **Stream**<br>• *Rock Creek* | **Watershed**<br>• *Clark Fork* |
| **Size**<br>• *Creek* | **Forest**<br>• *Beaverhead-Deerlodge* |
| **Height**<br>• *35 ft.* | **Hike**<br>• *1 mi. - Easy hike* |
| **Formation**<br>• *Cascade* | **Road access**<br>• *Difficult - 4 wheel drive* |
| **Elevation**<br>• *6138* | **Season**<br>• *Spring, Summer and Fall* |
| **Area**<br>• *Western* | **Latitude**<br>• *46.410212* |
| **County**<br>• *Powell* | **Longitude**<br>• *112.963142* |

From Deer Lodge, drive northwest on the Old Stage Road (County Road 006) for 5.6 miles to FR 168. Turn left onto FR 168, driving west for 6.9 miles to the end of Rock Creek Lake to a small parking area for TR 53.

*Rock Creek Lake*

## HISTORY

Grant-Kohrs Ranch National Historic Site is on the north end of the town of Deer Lodge. This ranch was started in 1863 by a Canadian fur trader named Johnny Grant. In 1866, Conrad Kohrs purchased the ranch, to raise beef for his gold-camp butcher shops. Eventually the herd grew to 50,000 head of cattle that purportedly grazed across 10 million acres of ranch and public land. Logically enough, Kohrs was given the nickname of Montana's Cattle King.

*Old mining shaft*

Old Montana Prison Museum is part of the Montana Prison Complex that includes Towe Ford Auto Museum, the Powell County Museum and the Frontier Montana Museum. The prison was the first territorial corrections facility built in the western United States. It was built by convict labor and completed in 1871, and when Montana became a state in 1889 it became the Montana State Prison. There were two notable prison riots, one in 1908 and the other in 1959, the first of which resulted in the death of Deputy Warden John Robinson, and the second that of Deputy Warden Theodore Rothe. The prison, overcrowded from the beginning, lasted over 100 years was replaced in 1979.

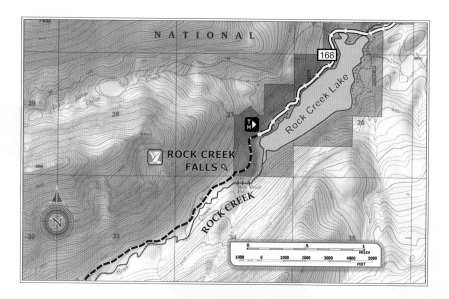

## CAMPING

**Rock Creek Campground** is a small undeveloped campground at the east end of Rock Creek Lake. Also there is a small undeveloped small camping space near the top of the falls (hike-in only).

**Racetrack Campground and Picnic Area** (USFS) is a pack in–pack out campground 11 miles west from the Racetrack exit (exit 195) off Interstate 90. There are 13 camping units, potable water and handicapped accessible vault toilets. This campground also has a picnic area and access to roaring Racetrack Creek. Camping is limited to 16 days and there is no fee.

## DESCRIPTION

This is a novel falls that is easily accessible. Usually only open for the summer months, the narrow Skalkaho dirt road winds up into the Sapphire Mountains through bear grass, huckleberries, and wildflowers. Suddenly you round a corner to find a tantalizing behemoth of a waterfall stretching out before you. Also noteworthy are the swarming crowds of people that seem to appear and disappear out of nowhere. Try to visit when there may not be as much traffic, such as weekdays in the summer or during fall and late spring. The falls is quite impressive with its height and cascading style. Be sure to check out Gem Mountain Sapphire Mine on the east side of Skalkaho Pass where you can pay to hunt sapphires.

*Skalkaho Falls*

| | |
|---|---|
| **Stream**<br>• Falls Creek | **Watershed**<br>• Bitterroot River |
| **Size**<br>• Creek | **Forest**<br>• Bitterroot National Forest |
| **Height**<br>• 150 ft. | **Hike**<br>• 0.1 mi. - short walk from road |
| **Formation**<br>• Cascade | **Road access**<br>• Dirt roads |
| **Elevation**<br>• 6319 | **Season**<br>• Summer |
| **Area**<br>• Western | **Latitude**<br>• 46.256203 |
| **County**<br>• Ravalli | **Longitude**<br>• -113.789349 |

## ACCESS

Drive south from Hamilton on US Highway 93 for 2.8 miles to Montana Secondary 38 (Skalkaho Highway). Turn left on the Skalkaho Highway for 24.1 miles, driving into the Sapphire Mountain Range, to the falls which are right off the road. Note: Skalkaho Highway may be closed in snowy weather!

*Elephant's head lousewort at Skalkaho Pass*

## HISTORY

The name "skalkaho" is believed to come from an Indian word meaning many roads. A story written by the founder of Grantsdale, H.H. Grant, on March 14, 1894 in the local paper, the Western News, alluded to the falls name and subsequent naming of nearby Skalkaho Creek.

The Bitterroot Mountains and the Bitterroot National Forest are named after the bitterroot plant, which is Montana's state flower. This plant was an important food source for the indigenous Indian tribes. The plant's root is very bitter in its raw form, but it was a fine meal when boiled and mixed with berries or meat. The boiled bitterroot was dried, pulverized and then seasoned with deer fat, berries, moss, and then molded into a patty, which were carried on hunting or war parties.

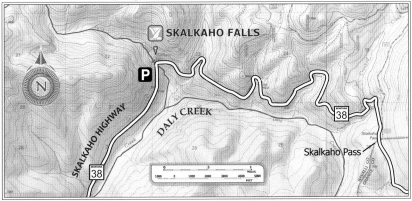

## CAMPING

**Black Bear Campground** (USFS) in the Bitterroot National Forest is located 13 miles east of US Highway 93 on the Skalkaho Highway (Montana Highway 38). This campground, at an elevation of 4,500', is adjacent to Skalkaho Creek and has 6 campsites, handicapped accessible toilets, no camping fee and a 14-day stay limit.

**Crystal Creek Campground** (USFS) is beautiful small alpine campground close to Mud Lake that is 31 miles southwest of Philipsburg on the Skalkaho Highway. There are only 3 campsites, 16-foot maximum trailer lengths, potable water, pack in–pack out rules, toilets and no camping fee.

Bitterroot National Forest
1801 North First Street
Hamilton, MT 59840
406-363-7100

# Snowshoe Falls

## DESCRIPTION

There is no defined trail, but after walking upstream from the turnout next to the highway for about 400 yards, you will see and hear Snowshoe Falls. It's a rare granite-based cascade that gushes through a crack and into a tight pool. Just 4 miles west a up the road is the historic Lolo Pass.

*Snowshoe Falls*

| | |
|---|---|
| **Stream**<br>• West Fork of Lolo Creek | **Watershed**<br>• Bitterroot River |
| **Size**<br>• Small stream | **Forest**<br>• Lolo National Forest |
| **Height**<br>• 20 ft. | **Hike**<br>• 0.5 mi. - short walk from road |
| **Formation**<br>• Cascade | **Road access**<br>• Easy highway/road access |
| **Elevation**<br>• 4603 | **Season**<br>• All |
| **Area**<br>• Western | **Latitude**<br>• 46.675384 |
| **County**<br>• Missoula | **Longitude**<br>• -114.57191 |

## ACCESS

From Lolo, Montana drive west on US Highway 12, paralleling Lolo Creek toward distant Lolo Pass. Just a half mile down the road is Travelers Rest State Park, an ancient Native American campsite used by Lewis and Clark in 1805 and on their return trip in 1806. Lolo Hot Springs, 29.3 miles farther up Highway 12, is a great place to soak and relax. Almost to the pass, at mile marker 5, is a highway turnout where can park. Walk on the creek side of the guard rail to the falls. Be careful—the highway here makes a sharp curve so there is limited visibility.

*Canada goldenrod*

## HISTORY

Travelers Rest State Park is the location of a Lewis and Clark Expedition campsite used in 1805 and 1806. By then, this site had been used for centuries by local Native Americans. In 2002, archaeologists found evidence of the group's latrine and main fire pit, marking Travelers Rest as one of the few sites in the nation with physical evidence of their encampment.

Fort Fizzle Historic Site Picnic Area is where, in July 1877, volunteers from nearby Missoula, led by Captain Rawn from Fort Missoula, erected a wooden barricade to halt the advance of an eastward-bound band of Nez Perce led by Hin-mah-too-yah-lat-kekt, or Chief Joseph, and others. The army gave Captain Rawn clear orders not to let the Nez Perce pass, but the barricade failed when the band climbed up a steep draw behind the ridge to the north and slipped around the soldiers. After the non-engagement, locals rather sarcastically named the site Fort Fizzle.

The Nez Perce men, women, children, and horse herd had crossed to this spot along the established Lolo Trail. This 200-mile stretch of tough mountainous terrain was developed by the Nez Perce and other tribes. The Shoshones introduced it to the Lewis and Clark Expedition, which followed it for 11 tormenting days. Distressed by frostbite, malnutrition, and dehydration, the crew pressed on to successfully cross into Idaho. The Lolo Trail is a National Historic Landmark and is administered by the National Park Service.

*Fort Fizzle informative sign*

## CAMPING

**Lolo Creek Campground** (USFS), at 3,800', is 15 miles west of Lolo on US Highway 12. Along the Lolo Trail, this campground has 17 campsites and 6 picnic areas. There are handicapped accessible toilets, potable water, trash pick-up, fishing and a $10/day camping fee. Earl Tennant Campground and Picnic Area (USFS), at 3,850', is 18

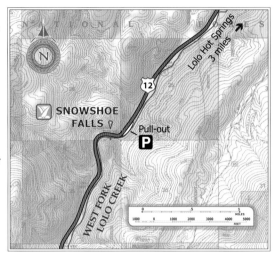

miles west of Lolo on US Highway 12. With segments of the historic Lolo Trail nearby, there are 6 double-wide campsites and a large picnic area. It has handicapped accessible toilets, trash pick-up, fishing and an $8/day camping fee.

**Lee Creek Campground** (USFS) is 26 miles west of Lolo, Montana on US Highway 12, sitting at 4,200' elevation. There are 22 campsites, handicapped accessible toilets, potable water, trash pick-up, and a $10/day camping fee.

Lolo National Forest
Fort Missoula Bldg. 24
Missoula, MT 59804
406-329-3750

*Fishing along Granite Creek*

## DESCRIPTION

Despite the multiple creek crossings and slightly misleading trail system at the beginning, this one will be a leading gem in your waterfalls-of-Montana accomplishments crown. Surrounded by the long-gone ghost forests set aflame by the Great Burn (also Great Fire) of 1910, Stepladder Falls pours over a series of ledges into green and gold pools. Downstream are myriad falls, drops, slides and micro-gorges. Many are remote and probably have been visited only a few times by humans. Be sure to check out Goldenrod Falls and First Gorge. Goldenrod is just downstream and around the corner from Stepladder. First Gorge lies where the trail nears the creek, and just upstream from the painfully inaccessible Lower Falls (briefly visible from the trail high above the valley's south). The dramatically folded golden-yellow sedimentary bedrock of the gorge is an unusual geological performance that is nearly unique to the stream beds in this area of Montana.

*Stepladder Falls*

| Stream | Watershed |
|---|---|
| • Straight Creek | • Clark Fork River |
| **Size** | **Forest** |
| • Creek | • Lolo National Forest |
| **Height** | **Hike** |
| • 60 ft. | • 11 mi. - Harder hike |
| **Formation** | **Road access** |
| • Terraced | • Dirt roads |
| **Elevation** | **Season** |
| • 4852 | • Spring, Summer and Fall |
| **Area** | **Latitude** |
| • Western | • 46.902464 |
| **County** | **Longitude** |
| • Mineral | • -114.898775 |

## ACCESS

From Alberton drive west 8.1 miles to exit 66 (Fish Creek). Take Exit 66 onto the Fish Creek Road (FR 343) and drive south for 10.9 miles to North Fork of Fish Creek Road. Take a right on FR 7750 (NF Fish Creek Road) driving west 5.8 miles to Clearwater Crossing Ranger Station and Campground. The trailhead for TR 99 going up Straight Creek starts at the end of the road. A half mile up the trail, make sure to take a left at the Straight Creek trail marker. You will cross the North Fork of Fish Creek and then Straight Creek—all in 50 yards—then, on land, locate the trail on the south bank of Straight Creek. (At this first crossing, avoid heading right and thus north on the deer trails somewhat enlarged by confused humans. People, including us, have tried to find our way to the main trail by incorrectly traversing the north side of the creek valley.) From the first crossing on the well worn (and correct) trail, head west up the canyon, cross the creek three more times before reaching Stepladder Falls.

## HISTORY

The Great Burn Proposed Wilderness Area is a 250,000-acre complex that encompasses areas in Idaho and Montana and is the newest proposed wilderness area in Montana. This pristine area was largely burned in the Great Burn's 3 million-acre conflagration. The Great Burn (or Great Fire) presents a prime example of a fire that burned segments of 10 national forests in Idaho, Montana and northeastern Washington, before burning into Canada. Today the area is a vibrant ecosystem including little pockets of 500-year-old western red cedar that survived the fire.

*Big pine tree*

*First gorge*

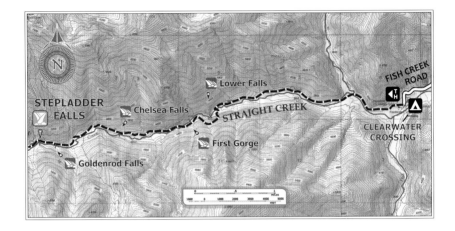

## CAMPING

**Clearwater Crossing Campground** (USFS) is a primitive pack in–pack out location. There are 3 campsites adjacent to the West Fork of Fish Creek, there also are a handicapped vault toilet, and potable water is available in the summer. This campground has stock facilities and offers access into the proposed Great Burn Wilderness Area. There is no fee at the Clearwater Crossing Campground, and the maximum stay is 14 days.

**Big Pine Campground and Fishing Access** (Montana Fish Wildlife and Parks) is a pack in–pack out campground with 5 campsites. There are a handicapped vault toilet, no potable water and no camping fee. The maximum stay is 7 days, and this campground offers access to magnificent Fish Creek. The largest pine tree of Montana — in this case ponderosa pine — is located at the southwest corner of the campground next to Fish Creek.

Montana Fish, Wildlife & Parks
Parks Division
406-444-3750

*Goldenrod Falls*

## DESCRIPTION

This is a classic Bitterroot Range hike and waterfall destination. You start out on private land (thanks to an easement) and just below a rock quarry. The trail climbs for a while, levels out somewhat then snakes between troll-like boulders covered in moss. Many of the big rocks are part of a newly developed bouldering area. (Some of the "problems," or bouldering routes, are quite stout with V-scale ratings ranging from V4 to V9, or higher.) Farther up is a burned-out area followed by a climb and then the falls. A good vantage point can be found below the falls. Watch out near the top because the ground slopes down to "Dante's disco party"—an "event" that you'll want to miss. There are more bedrock waterslides and waterfall action above here. Be sure to check them out.

*Sweathouse Creek Falls*

| Stream | Watershed |
|---|---|
| • *Sweathouse Creek* | • *Bitterroot River* |
| **Size** | **Forest** |
| • *Creek* | • *Bitterroot National Forest* |
| **Height** | **Hike** |
| • *75 ft.* | • *3 mi. - Moderate hike* |
| **Formation** | **Road access** |
| • *Tiered* | • *Dirt roads* |
| **Elevation** | **Season** |
| • *5217* | • *Spring, Summer and Fall* |
| **Area** | **Latitude** |
| • *Western* | • *46.424531* |
| **County** | **Longitude** |
| • *Ravalli* | • *-114.256478* |

## ACCESS

Head west from Victor on Sweathouse Creek Road for 2.8 miles to its end. There is a small parking area for the trailhead to TR 121, which goes up Sweathouse Creek in the Bitterroot Mountains.

*Backside of the Bitterroot Mountains*

## HISTORY

Fort Owen State Park is the site of the first white settlement in Montana. Established in 1850, it was named after Major John Owens. Made of adobe and logs, the fort also served as a trading post for the early pioneers, missionaries and the Indians of the Bitterroot Valley. Parts of the fort's original permanent structures still stand in the park.

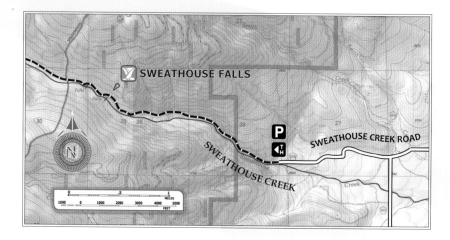

## CAMPING

**Blodgett Creek Campground** (USFS), 4.1 miles from Hamilton, is a small pack in–pack out campground. There are 7 campsites available and the site is equipped with restrooms.

**Charles Waters Memorial Campground** (USFS) is up Bass Creek Road 2.1 miles from US Highway 93, some 4 miles south of Florence. Located just inside the Bitterroot National Forest boundary, the campground has 28 campsites, potable water and wheelchair accessible restrooms, with a $10/day fee. Charles Waters Memorial CG is open from April 1 till November 1.

Bitterroot National Forest
1801 North First Street
Hamilton, MT 59840
406-363-7100

# Montana Waterfalls Northcentral Region

## DESCRIPTION

When you come across this golden-yellow falls, you will be surprised at how quickly it appears. This waterfall has several levels — the top is the largest and most dramatic plunge, while the lower part is reckless cascades. Take note of the stunning amount of greenery around the area. This is typical of the Swan Valley — lush forests, huckleberries, bears, hidden waterfalls and road-less areas.

*Arnica Falls*

| | |
|---|---|
| **Stream** | **Wate** |
| • North Fork of Lost Creek | • Swa |
| **Size** | **Fores** |
| • Small stream | • Flathead National Forest |
| **Height** | **Hike** |
| • 130 ft. | • 0.5 mi. - short walk from road |
| **Formation** | **Road access** |
| • Cascade | • Dirt Roads |
| **Elevation** | **Season** |
| • 4630 | • Spring and Summer |
| **Area** | **Latitude** |
| • Northcentral | • 47.901608 |
| **County** | **Longitude** |
| • Lake | • -113.711421 |

ACCESS

From Big Fork, head east on Montana Highway 209 (State High-way 209) 5.3 miles to MT-83. Turn right at MT-83 and continue south for about 13 miles. Turn left at Lost Creek Road (National Forest Development Road 680) and follow this road for about 2.5 miles. A quarter mile after the road crosses the creek, stay left as the road forks and follow National Forest Road 5206 for 4 miles. When you come to a sharp switchback in the road, park and walk or bike along an old logging road heading east for a quarter mile until the path crosses a side stream. The falls can be viewed by looking up to the north.

## ...ORY

...west of Arnica Falls is
...wan Lake and the Swan
... Valley. The lake is beautiful
...d clean. It stretches lengthwise
for quite some distance while aver-
aging only a mile in width. At the
south end of the lake, you will find
a little paradise at the Swan River
National Wildlife Refuge. Board-
walks give you a wide view of
thriving marshlands and a healthy
variety of native birds and other
critters.

To the North of Swan Lake is
the town of Bigfork, famous for its
'Wild Mile' Whitewater Festival,
bustling micro artist community
and over-the-top real estate values.
It's worth the trip to Bigfork, as
this small town overlooking Flathead Lake is strikingly beautiful.

*Below Arnica Falls*

## GEOLOGY

Glaciers moving south down the Flathead valley ground down the northern finger of the Mission Mountains just south of Bigfork. This is evident by the rounding of the hills and mountains and glacial scraping in the area. The falls flows over tan and grey upthrusts of belt series rock forming the Swan Range. The Swans are nearly a mirror image of the Mission Mountains to the west, and form an unbroken north to south line of tilted, primarily Precambrian mudstone formed nearly a billion years ago.

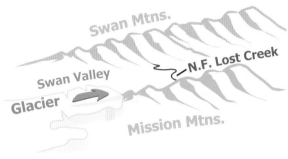

## CAMPING

**Swan Lake Campground** is about 9 miles from the falls. It sits near the south end of Swan Lake, has 36 campsites, restrooms, laundry facilities, is handicap-accessible, and provides a boat launch. Swimming and fishing is available and pets are welcome. Fees for the use of the campground are $14 per day for individual campsites, $25 per year for a pass or $3 per day for day use, $25 per night for group site overnight use, and $75 per day for group site day use. Maximum stay is limited to 14 days.

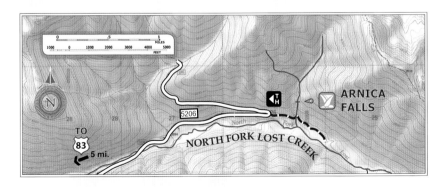

# Baring Falls

## DESCRIPTION

This is one of our favorites in Glacier National Park. The water pours at an angle onto a smooth, red wall of Precambrian mudstone, and then rushes for about 50 yards, where it then empties into St. Mary's Lake. It's a quick 15-minute hike from the road and a 30-minute tour boat ride on St. Mary's Lake to where the stream flows into the lake. There are many waterfalls on this creek. Three richly colored, green, stone waterfalls are right in the vicinity of the Sunrift Gorge parking area. If you hike 100 yards upstream from Sunrift Gorge, you will come across a series of deep, red, punch-bowl style waterfalls. About 1 mile up the trail is another breathtaking falls with glacier-carved mountain views of the Baring Creek Valley. Enjoy.

*Baring Falls*

| | |
|---|---|
| **Stream**<br>• Baring Creek | **Watershed**<br>• St. Mary River |
| **Size**<br>• Small stream | **Forest**<br>• Glacier National Park |
| **Height**<br>• 30 ft. | **Hike**<br>• 1/2 mi. - Easy hike |
| **Formation**<br>• Shoestring | **Road access**<br>• Easy highway/road access |
| **Elevation**<br>• 4564 | **Season**<br>• Summer and Fall |
| **Area**<br>• Northcentral | **Latitude**<br>• 48.676935 |
| **County**<br>• Glacier | **Longitude**<br>• -114.814626 |

## ACCESS

From the town of St. Mary, travel west on Going-to-the-Sun Road for 10.5 miles to the Sunrift pullout. Park at Sunrift Gorge or the alternate pull-out a little further up the road and walk back down to Sunrift Gorge. From the gorge, hike the trail for 15 minutes down to the falls and the lake.

Note: This road may be closed seasonally.

*Black bear near the entrance of the park*

## HISTORY

Sunrift Gorge is a curious place. It is a deep, straight, vertical gorge that holds Baring Creek, the source for Baring Falls and other waterfalls. Unlike many gorges, Sunrift was not formed by erosion. After a section of ice melted, the massive block of rock that sat beneath the hillside to the south broke away and moved a few feet downhill. The creek then re-routed and found its new course through the new, narrow slot.

*Below Sunrift Gorge*                    *Sunrift Gorge*

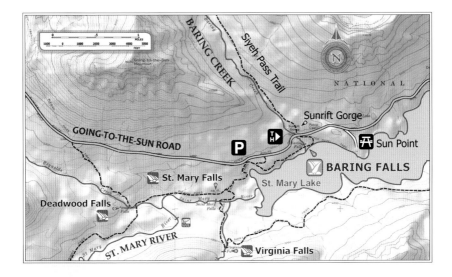

## CAMPING

Rising Sun (Glacier National Park) is an excellent campground that is located where they say "the mountains meet the prairies." There are numerous waterfalls located 2 miles up Rose Creek. To get there, start hiking from the campground and keep an eye out for bears. The campground is just west of the town of St. Mary and halfway along St. Mary's Lake on the north side of Going-to-the-Sun Road.

**St. Mary's campground** (Glacier National Park) is the largest on the east side of the park. Located a half-mile from the St. Mary's Visitor Center, this splendid place has a few extra amenities that many campgrounds lack, such as flushing toilets.

There is also camping at the KOA just outside of the town of St. Mary.

**Glacier National Park**
P.O. Box 128
West Glacier, MT 59936
406-888-7800

# Black Eagle Falls

## DESCRIPTION

The first falls along the Great Falls corridor of the Missouri River is Black Eagle, a multi-step cascade with several sheer drops. Both sides of the river have trails and offer public access. You can get closest to the falls on the north side. There is a hydroelectric dam on this side, along with a full-size, out-of-commission turbine blade. A couple hundred feet downstream are rapids that make a great play spot for kayakers. If you are on the island below the falls, the play spot is located near the downstream tip.

Be sure to also visit Giant Springs and Rainbow Falls. The latter is as beautiful as Black Eagle Falls and comes complete with a surprise drop, a hidden falls, just downstream.

*Black Eagle Falls*

## SUMMARY

| | |
|---|---|
| **Stream**<br>• Missouri River | **Watershed**<br>• Missouri River |
| **Size**<br>• Large river | **Forest**<br>• Lewis & Clark National Forest |
| **Height**<br>• 26 ft. | **Hike**<br>• 0 mi. - short walk from road |
| **Formation**<br>• Terraced | **Road access**<br>• Easy highway/road access |
| **Elevation**<br>• 3251 | **Season**<br>• Spring |
| **Area**<br>• Central | **Latitude**<br>• 47.520179 |
| **County**<br>• Cascade | **Longitude**<br>• 111.261896 |

## ACCESS

From downtown Great Falls take 15th St. NE (Highway 87) north and over the bridge. Once you've cleared the river, take the first right on N River Rd. Continue for about 1/2 mile to where the road dips down to the power station and parking area. To get to Rainbow Falls starting at Black Eagle Falls on the south side of the river follow River Dr. N for 1/2 mile, take a left at Giant Springs Rd and continue for about 1 1/2 miles until you reach the Rainbow Falls trailhead on the left. Bike or hike eastward on a well made trail to access the bottom of Crooked Falls.

## HISTORY

When Caption Meriwether Lewis first came to the Great Falls of the Missouri, he walked down the 200-foot bluff to the river bottom and out to a rock point. From there, he gazed up the spectacle and exclaimed that it was the grandest sight he ever saw. Lewis soon learned that there were four more magnificent waterfalls upstream along this 12-mile stretch of the River. It took Lewis, William Clark and their crew of hardy, courageous men a month to portage their boats and gear 18.5 miles around all of the falls.

Giant Springs State Park is located just outside of the city of Great Falls on Giant Springs Road. This is one of the country's largest freshwater springs. It was discovered in 1805 when the "Corps of Discovery" (explain who they areLewis and Clark Expedition) were camped below the Great Falls, preparing to portage around them. Giant Springs discharges around 57 billion gallons of drinkable water annually. The fish hatchery connected to the springs raises about 750,000 fish each year that are distributed around the state. Giant Springs is the most visited state park in Montana.

*Great Falls of the Missouri River by F. Jay Haynes, summer 1880 (Montana Historical Society)*

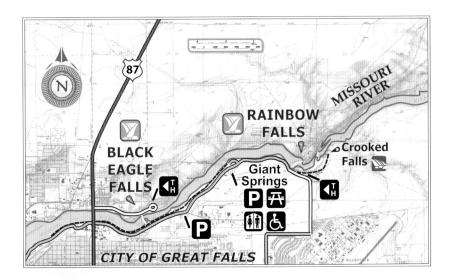

## CAMPING

There are quite a few private campgrounds in or around the city of Great Falls.

Giant Springs State Park
4600 Giant Springs Road
Great Falls, MT 59405
406-454-5840

# Double Falls

## DESCRIPTION

The trailhead starts at the northwest end of Double Falls Campground. Walking upstream next to Ford Creek on an undeveloped nature trail a mere 200 yards will lead you to Double Falls, a rugged plunging cascade.

*Double Falls*

| | |
|---|---|
| **Stream**<br>• Ford Creek | **Watershed**<br>• Sun River |
| **Size**<br>• Creek | **Forest**<br>• Lewis & Clark National Forest |
| **Height**<br>• 70 ft. | **Hike**<br>• 0.75 mi. - Short walk |
| **Formation**<br>• Tiered | **Road access**<br>• Dirt roads |
| **Elevation**<br>• 5425 | **Season**<br>• Spring, Summer and Fall |
| **Area**<br>• Central | **Latitude**<br>• 47.404304 |
| **County**<br>• Lewis and Clark | **Longitude**<br>• -112.735562 |

### ACCESS

From Augusta, head west on the Augusta Ranger Station Road 13 miles to Benchmark Road. Turn left and drive southwest on Benchmark Road for 5.1 miles to Double Falls Campground.

*Northern goshawk*

### HISTORY

The Bob Marshall Wilderness, the Great Bear Wilderness and the Scapegoat Wilderness collectively forms the Bob Marshall Wilderness Complex. This was all started in 1964, when the United States Congress passed the first Wilderness Act. The Bob Marshall Wilderness Area was part of the original act of 1964, with the complex presently spanning an area of over 1.5 million acres.

Robert "Bob" Marshall was born in 1901 and passed away a short 39 years later. A prolific writer, he wrote fervently on all aspects of conservation and preservation. He was the principal founder of The Wilderness Society and helped shape the U.S. Forest Service policy on wilderness designation.

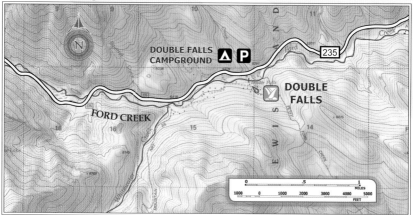

### CAMPING

**Double Falls Campground** (USFS) is a small 3 unit pack in–pack out campsite. There is a toilet, no water, and no fee.

**Wood Lake Campground** (USFS) is another 6 miles up Benchmark Road. It offers 9 camping units with tables, potable water, toilets, and a camping fee. Activities could include: fishing, hiking, canoeing, and swimming.

**Benchmark Campground** (USFS) is 6 miles past Wood Lake Campground on Benchmark Road. It has 25 campsites with tables, potable water, toilets, and a daily camping fee. Activities could include fishing, hiking, and horseback riding, also there's an adjacent airfield, and a Bob Marshall Wilderness Complex trailhead starts from this campground.

Lewis And Clark National Forest
1101 15th Street N.
Great Falls, MT 59401
406-791-7700

# Holland Falls

## DESCRIPTION

The trailhead for 1.5-mile-long Holland Falls National Recreation Trail starts at the end of Holland Lake Road. At the start of TR 416 you walk through mixed stands of western larch, ponderosa pine and red fir, viewing an unbelievable Holland Lake that's so serene, so beautiful. Almost a mile along, the trail starts to climb at a steady grade up rocky slopes. A little farther along you will come to a footbridge, crossing a small, sparkling mountain brook. Hiking another couple hundred yards up the trail, along the mountainside, you come to rock outcroppings that allow panoramic views of the Swan Valley, Swan Mountain Range and the Mission Mountains. Hearing the falls now, you hike only a short distance before seeing the striking sight of Holland Falls as it hurls itself down a tight canyon.

*Holland Falls*

SUMMARY

| | |
|---|---|
| **Stream**<br>• Holland Creek | **Watershed**<br>• Swan River |
| **Size**<br>• Creek | **Forest**<br>• Lolo National Forest |
| **Height**<br>• 55 ft. | **Hike**<br>• 2.25 mi. - Easy hike |
| **Formation**<br>• Horsetail | **Road access**<br>• Easy highway/road access |
| **Elevation**<br>• 5059 | **Season**<br>• Summer |
| **Area**<br>• Northwest | **Latitude**<br>• 47.450786 |
| **County**<br>• Missoula | **Longitude**<br>• -113.571682 |

## ACCESS

Travel from Seely Lake north on Montana Highway 83 for 20.8 miles to Holland Lake Road. Turn right, traveling east on the gravel Holland Lake Road 2.9 miles to pass Larch Loop Campground and continue another 0.75 of a mile to the Bay Loop Compound turn-in, where the trail starts.

*Rocky Mountain blazing star*

## HISTORY

Something like 10,000 years ago, the Ice Age ended with a sudden warming change in climate. After less than 3,000 years the mass of ice that filled the Swan Valley had disappeared, leaving the out-wash sediments and forming the current valley floor. Smaller glaciers still continued to creep down the valleys of the Missions and Swan after the mass of ice was gone. The last glacial lobes of ice left high moraines around their edges that now enfold Holland Lake and Lindbergh Lake, as with quite a few other lakes at the apertures of any sizable canyons in the Missions and Swan ranges.

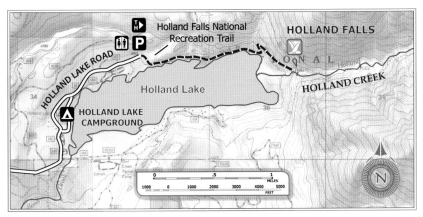

## CAMPING

**Holland Lake Campground** (USFS) is located right on Holland Lake, and has two loops. First is Larch Loop, which is on a small bluff overlooking the lake. The second loop, a little more than three-fourths of the way down Holland Lake Road, is called Bay Loop. This campground is situated around a gorgeous little bay. Combined there are 39 camping units, drinking water, trash pickup, toilet facilities and a $12/day fee with two weeks maximum stay. This is Grizzly Bear coun-tryyou must know and practice safe food-storage techniques.

**Lindbergh Lake Campground** (USFS elevation 4367') is a pack in–pack out campground. There are 22 campsites available, wheelchair accessible restrooms, fishing access and boat ramp access to Lindbergh Lake. The vista with the lake and Mission Mountains is special.

Flathead National Forest
650 Wolfpack Way
Kalispell, MT 59901
406-758-5200

# Mill Falls

## DESCRIPTION

The trailhead to Mill Falls is accessed at Mill Falls Campground. The hike to the falls is an easy 200-yard walk through a forest of tall Engelmann spruce and grand black cottonwood trees. At the end of the trail, Mill Falls cascades down into a shallow, crystal-clear pool.

*Mill Falls*

## SUMMARY

| Stream | Watershed |
| --- | --- |
| • South Fork of the Teton River | • Missouri River |
| **Size** | **Forest** |
| • Small stream | • Lewis & Clark National Forest |
| **Height** | **Hike** |
| • 75 ft. | • 0.6 mi. - Easy hike |
| **Formation** | **Road access** |
| • Shoestring | • Dirt roads |
| **Elevation** | **Season** |
| • 5699 | • Spring, Summer |
| **Area** | **Latitude** |
| • Northcentral | • 47.868315 |
| **County** | **Longitude** |
| • Teton | • -112.757449 |

### ACCESS

From Choteau, travel northwest on US Highway 89 5.2 miles to Canyon Road. Turn left onto Canyon Road, driving west into the awesome Eastern Front of the Rocky Mountains. Travel 16.8 miles to the Bellview Teton Road. Turn left on it and drive 0.4 mile to Loop Road, where you turn right. Take Loop Road another 0.4 mile to South Fork Road. Continue on the South Fork Road (FR 109) 7.2 miles to Mill Falls Campground turnoff and the Mill Falls trailhead.

*Beaver Dam at the Middle Fork Teton River*

## HISTORY

The Rocky Mountain Front is the awesome formation of steep rugged mountains and deep canyons at the edge of the Great Plains that extends from Glacier National Park southward to about Rogers Pass. The transformation from the mountainous heights to the foothills, which then open onto the immense expanse of Montana's grasslands and prairie, is striking.

This change from peak to prairie produces an ecological transition zone or ecozone that yields a sanctuary supporting an amazing diversity of wildlife. This key habitat is home to elk, bighorn sheep, mountain goat, black bear, grizzly bear, mountain lion, badger, bobcat, Canadian lynx, red fox, wolverine, coyote, beaver, marten, moose, mule deer and whitetail deer, to name some species.

One of the oldest trails along the eastern front of the Rookies was called 'miisum Apatosiosoko' or the Ancient North Trail, by the Blackfeet Indians. Evidence of the trail route is visible in the form of remaining small rock cairns. Archaeologists believe this route of travel, along the eastern front of the Rockies, is indicative of the earliest migrations of people into the New World from Siberia about 25,000 years ago. The Old Trail Museum in Choteau has information regarding the trail.

Informative markers for the Old North Trail can be found along the trail at:
- Choteau — Travel 20 miles west of Highway 89 on North Fork of the Teton Road and on South Fork of the Teton Road.
- Bynum — Travel west of Highway 89 on Blackleaf Road.
- Dupuyer — Travel 17 miles west of Highway 89 on Swift Dam Road.

*Part of the Rocky Mountain Front*

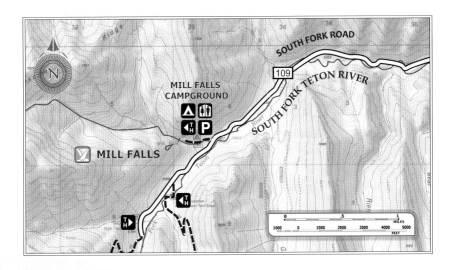

## CAMPING

**Mill Falls Campground** (USFS) is 33.8 miles northwest of Choteau in the Lewis and Clark National Forest. There are 4 camping units, toilet facilities, no drinking water, no fees and a pack in–pack out policy.

Lewis And Clark National Forest
1101 15th Street N.
Great Falls, MT 59401
406-791-7700

## DESCRIPTION

This is really two falls in one. During high water, the water leaps from the top shelf, hiding a second falls that roars out of a cave halfway down. During low-water flow, water gushes from the cave only, leaving the top dry. However, at any water level this is a phenomenal place to be. As you approach the falls, notice the unusual warping of the surrounding sedimentary rocks. This formation is from the relatively unusual action of older rocks sliding over younger rocks, which is common in and around Glacier National Park.

*Running Eagle Falls*

| Stream | Watershed |
|---|---|
| • Two Medicine River | • Missouri River |
| **Size** | **Forest** |
| • River | • Glacier National Park |
| **Height** | **Hike** |
| • 40 ft. | • 0.5 mi. - short walk from road |
| **Formation** | **Road access** |
| • Sheer falls | • Easy highway/road access |
| **Elevation** | **Season** |
| • 5046 | • Spring, Summer and Fall |
| **Area** | **Latitude** |
| • Northcentral | • 48.497953 |
| **County** | **Longitude** |
| • Glacier | • -113.351912 |

## ACCESS

From the town of East Glacier, drive north on Highway 49 for 4.1 miles to Two Medicine Road. Take a left onto Two Medicine Road following the northern shore line of Lower Two Medicine Lake for 6.4 miles. Just as the road crosses the Two Medicine River and starts to head south, pull into the small parking lot on the right. The trail is around 0.3 mile long and is wheelchair accessible.

*Leafy Aster*

## HISTORY

This falls is named after Running Eagle (Pitamakan), a Blackfeet woman who lived around 1825. As the story goes, she gravitated to the skills of a Blackfeet warrior. She became a great hunter and was incredibly brave in the face of her tribe's enemies. At one point, Running Eagle was instructed by the village elders to go on a vision quest in order to find her true calling. It is said that she went on the quest near these falls. Running Eagle told of her adventures in medicine lodge ceremonies while becoming a member of the Braves Society of young warriors. She continued to lead—successfully—war and hunting parties until she died in a battle against a party of Flatheads near the Sun River.

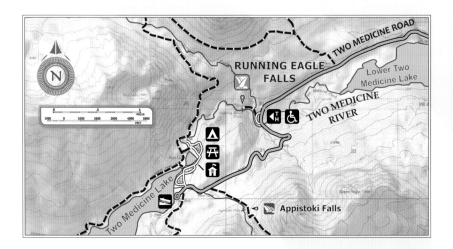

## CAMPING

**Two Medicine Campground** is located at the edge of serene Two Medicine Lake. There are 99 campsites, potable water, and the restrooms have flush toilets and sinks with running water. Campsites are first-come, first-served with summer operation from May 28 to September 19 and primitive operation from September 20 to October 31. Two Medicine Campground also offers, during the summer, nightly amphitheater programs by park rangers. Fees are: summer operation $20.00/night; primitive camping $10.00/night.

Glacier National Park
P.O. Box 128
West Glacier, MT 59936
406-888-7800

# St. Mary Falls

## DESCRIPTION

St. Mary Falls is a fantastic destination for hikers. Rimmed with richly colored red rocks and vibrant moss, this treasure is a recreational high point for hikers within the east side of Glacier National Park. The upper section of the falls makes a dramatic entrance by tumbling through a narrow slot then terminating against the south wall. Soon after is the main falls, which makes a clean leap from its colorful surroundings. Take notice of the color of the water as it swirls downstream. It is a brilliant turquoise green with a hint of blue. This is due to glacial sediments mixing with snow and glacial melt. A little farther downstream, the river empties into St. Mary Lake. Various tour-boat rides on the lake can extend your hiking and camping experiences. Be sure to check local schedules for this service.

*St. Mary Falls*

SUMMARY

| Stream | Watershed |
|---|---|
| • St. Mary River | • St. Mary River |
| **Size** | **Forest** |
| • River | • Glacier National Park |
| **Height** | **Hike** |
| • 40 ft. | • 2 mi. - Easy hike |
| **Formation** | **Road access** |
| • Terraced | • Easy highway/road access |
| **Elevation** | **Season** |
| • 4606 | • Spring, Summer and Fall |
| **Area** | **Latitude** |
| • Northcentral | • 48.667782 |
| **County** | **Longitude** |
| • Glacier | • -113.615928 |

## ACCESS

From St. Mary drive west 11.0 miles to the trailhead. Many Falls Trail heads just under a mile west of Sunrift Gorge and is located on the south side of the Going-to-the-Sun Road. This is an 0.8-mile hike with an elevation drop of 150'. If you have the time and energy, be sure to check out Virginia and Deadwood falls. They are both within short hiking distances from St Mary Falls.

*Below the falls*

## HISTORY

In 1921, work began on Going-to-the-Sun Road, an automobile route that would connect West Glacier to Logan Pass on the Continental Divide and proceed on to St. Mary Lake on the park's east side. By 1932, after years of grueling labor carving the highway from the mighty Garden Wall cliffs, the road was finally finished. Its engineers rejected the typical multiple switchbacks road style (common in the Alps of Europe), and instead they designed a route requiring only two major turns.

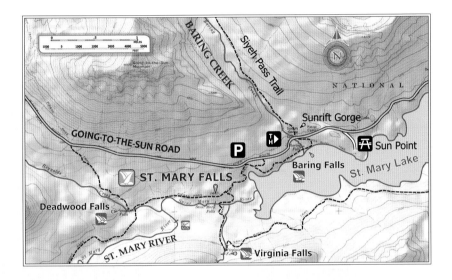

## CAMPING

**Rising Sun Campground** is a great campground that is located where they say "the mountains meet the prairies." This spot is just west of the town of St. Mary and halfway along St. Mary Lake on the north side of the Going-to-the-Sun Road.

**St. Mary Campground** is the largest campground on the east side of the park. Located one half mile from the St. Mary Visitor Center, this splendid place has a few extra amenities that many campgrounds lack (flush toilets, etc.).

Glacier National Park
P.O. Box 128
West Glacier, MT 59936
406-888-7800

## DESCRIPTION

If you are spending time at the Many Glacier Hotel or on your way to Swiftcurrent Lake, be sure to stop and see Swiftcurrent Falls. This multi-pitched cascade can be very photogenic with its golden-yellow rock and towering Mount Grinnell backdrop. Notably, the falls is formed from the same upturned limestone bedrock the holds back the waters of Swiftcurrent Lake.

*Swiftcurrent Falls*

SUMMARY

| | |
|---|---|
| **Stream**<br>• Swiftcurrent Creek | **Watershed**<br>• Swiftcurrent Creek |
| **Size**<br>• Creek | **Forest**<br>• Glacier National Park |
| **Height**<br>• 50 ft. | **Hike**<br>• 0.1 mi. - short walk from road |
| **Formation**<br>• Terraced | **Road access**<br>• Easy highway/road access |
| **Elevation**<br>• 4797 | **Season**<br>• Spring, Summer and Fall |
| **Area**<br>• Northcentral | **Latitude**<br>• 48.799967 |
| **County**<br>• Glacier | **Longitude**<br>• -113.649702 |

## ACCESS

From Babb, drive into the pristine beauty of Glacier National Park on US Highway 89 south for 0.3 miles. Turn right onto Many Glacier Road for 11.4 miles to the Many Glacier Hotel. Lake Sherburne is adjacent to the road for most of the way, contributing more unbelievable scenic views of the park. Just north of the hotel is parking for the trailhead to Swiftcurrent Falls. The falls can be viewed either from the roadway or from the trail's viewing areas.

*Eastern front near Swiftcurrent Falls*

## HISTORY

In 1932, Glacier Park and Canada's Waterton Lakes National Park were designated Waterton–Glacier International Peace Park. Glacier and Waterton Lake parks both have been tabbed as Biosphere Reserves, and together are recognized in 1995 as World Heritage sites.

## GEOLOGY

In 1923, witherite—an uncommon carbonate mineral—was discovered filling cavities in the Altyn limestone of the Belt Series rock in Glacier National Park. The main exposures show in the lower belt of limestone right above the Lewis Overthrust fault along the gorge below Swiftcurrent Falls. Altyn limestone is a highly siliceous calcium-magnesium-carbonate rock containing rounded to angular quartz and feldspar grains, which in a weathered surface is light brown and dotted with etched grains of sand.

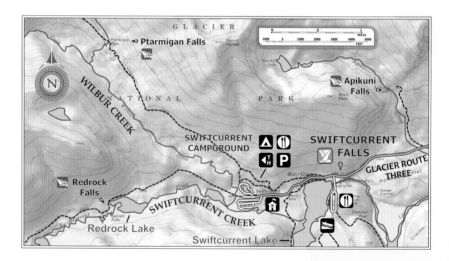

## CAMPING

**Many Glacier Campground** (GNP) has 110 campsites with 35 reserved for RV's with a maximum length of 35 feet. At the campground there are a store, showers, potable water, handicapped accessible toilets, and a $14/day camping fee.

Glacier National Park
P.O. Box 128
West Glacier, MT 59936
406-888-7800

# Montana Waterfalls Central Region

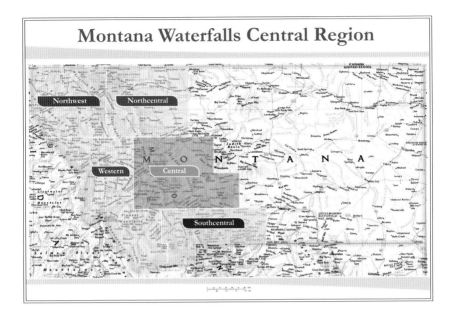

# Cataract Falls

## DESCRIPTION

From the small parking area adjacent to sparkling Elk Creek, cross over the creek (there is no bridge) to the start of an undeveloped trail. Follow this trail 400 yards uphill, winding though a nice pine and fir forest to the base of this wonderful, cascading waterfall.

*Cataract Falls*

SUMMARY

| Stream | Watershed |
|---|---|
| • Cataract Creek | • Sun River |
| **Size** | **Forest** |
| • Small stream | • Lewis & Clark National Forest |
| **Height** | **Hike** |
| • 90 ft. | • 0.5 mi. - short walk from road |
| **Formation** | **Road access** |
| • Shoestring | • Dirt roads |
| **Elevation** | **Season** |
| • 5387 | • Spring, Summer and Fall |
| **Area** | **Latitude** |
| • Northcentral | • 47.322447 |
| **County** | **Longitude** |
| • Lewis and Clark | • -112.604027 |

### ACCESS

From Augusta, drive southwest on the Augusta Stearns Road 6.3 miles. Turn right on Elk Creek Road and head southwest for 10.1 miles. On the left, next to Elk Creek, is a small parking area. You must cross the creek to get to the trailhead.

*Scarlet paintbrush*

## HISTORY

The Ancient North Trail, as the Blackfeet Tribe called it, follows the eastern front of the Rocky Mountains. The Blackfeet used it on travels from their northern hunting grounds of the summer to their winter encampments in the south. Prior to the Blackfeet, ancient groups of people, traveling south, used the trail possibly as far back as 25,000 years ago. Today it's known as the Old North Trail.

Just west of here, in the small town of Cascade, Charles M. Russell (1864-1926), one of the more famous American western artists, spent the early years of a career that produced 2,600 pieces of art. He grew up in St. Louis, Ill., and in 1880, at the age of 15, came to Montana. Russell quit his first job as a sheepherder because it wasn't quite what he had expected of living and working on the western frontier. In the summer of 1881, he was out of food and money and rode his horse aimlessly out near the Judith River. He camped just off the riverside. As fate would have it, Jake Hoover, a local prospector, meat hunter and trapper, set up camp next to him. For the next two years, Charlie Russell and Jake Hoover traveled through wilderness, taking it all in. These experiences on the eastern front of the Rocky Mountains inspired Russell's later artwork. He developed a deep love for Montana and its native and im-migrant populations.

*Miner's cabin*

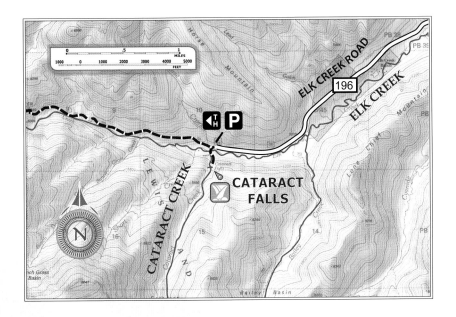

## CAMPING

**Bean Lake** is a fishing access site run by Montana Fish, Wildlife and Parks. From Augusta, drive southwest 15 miles on the Stearns Augusta Road, and you will reach this small lake with a concrete boat launch. There is a handicapped-accessible toilet with 50 primitive campsites. No drinking water is available. The maximum stay is seven days. Fish, Wildlife and Parks camping is $12.00 (without a Montana fishing license) and $7.00 (with Montana fishing license).

Montana Fish, Wildlife and Parks
Parks Division
406-444-3750

## DESCRIPTION

From the trailhead of TR 109 you start switch-backing down to Hall Creek, then crossing over and into Crow Creek drainage. Not very far along the trail becomes rocky and steep in places. At the confluence of Dewey Creek you start climbing out of the draw up to hillsides of ponderosa pine and Douglas-fir. Signs of old gold mining activities can be seen along this historic trail as you swing back to the creek and the faint roar of the falls. At the end of this 3.5-mile hike is Crow Creek Falls, flowing over an ancient rock formation dropping 40 feet into a crystalline pool.

*Crow Creek Falls*

| | |
|---|---|
| **Stream**<br>• Crow Creek | **Watershed**<br>• Missouri River |
| **Size**<br>• Creek | **Forest**<br>• Helena National Forest |
| **Height**<br>• 45 ft. | **Hike**<br>• 7 mi. - Moderate hike |
| **Formation**<br>• Punchbowl | **Road access**<br>• Rough roads at times |
| **Elevation**<br>• 5917 | **Season**<br>• Spring, Summer and Fall |
| **Area**<br>• Central | **Latitude**<br>• 46.330839 |
| **County**<br>• Jefferson | **Longitude**<br>• -111.776748 |

## ACCESS

From Townsend travel north on US Highway 12 for one mile. Turn left on Indian Creek Road driving west into the Elkhorn Mountains for 11.5 miles to FR 4031. Turn left onto Wave Road (FR 4031) for 2.5 miles to FR 424. Turn right on FR 424 for one mile to an unimproved campground and Trailhead 109.

*Crow Creek Trail*

## HISTORY

Crow Creek Falls is part of the historic Hawkeye placer mine which was patented in the early 1920s. In 2002, a non-profit group, American Land Conservancy, purchased the parcel. In partner-

ship with the Montana Mining Association and the Montana Wilderness Association they are now in the process of cleaning up the old mining debris and equipment and are reclaiming this unique recreational destination.

The Hawkeye patent is within a large roadless portion of the Elkhorn Wildlife Management Unit and Crow Creek is the largest

*Century-old mining office*

watershed in the unit. Crow Creek Falls is a major natural feature and its area a sanctuary for many wildlife species, including the threatened Canadian lynx, the sensitive goshawk and west slope cutthroat trout.

*Kleinschmidt Mine in the Elkhorn Mountains*

## GEOLOGY

Crow Creek drainage is a fifty-million-year-old Mesozoic rock layered with Cretaceous sandstone and shale.

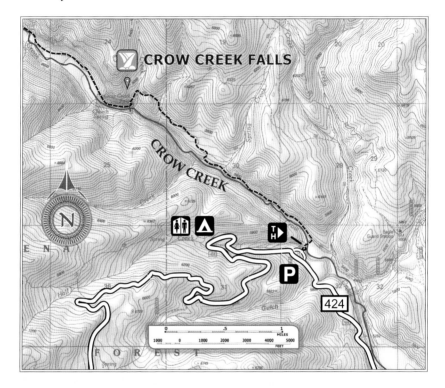

## CAMPING

**There are undeveloped campsites** about 1.5 miles from Crow Creek Falls' trailhead. At the trailhead is another undeveloped campsite area with toilet facilities.

**Eagle Creek Guard Station** (USFS) is one of eight cabins and guard stations that are available through Helena National Forest rental program. To stay at Eagle Guard Station costs $25/day for up to six people, with the maximum stay of 5 days.

Helena National Forest
2880 Skyway Drive
Helena, MT 59602
406-449-5201

## DESCRIPTION

The Dearborn River carves through dramatic rock formations along its length, especially through Devils Glen. The first set of cascades is around 2 miles upstream from the trailhead where the trail comes back down to the creek. They are a beautiful series of small drops and deep blue-green pools. Farther upstream and along the trail is Devils Glen, a magnificent display of water-shaped rock and sporadic falls under 12 feet in height.

*Dearborn River Cascades*

## SUMMARY

| Stream | Watershed |
|---|---|
| • Dearborn River | • Missouri River |
| **Size** | **Forest** |
| • River | • Lewis & Clark National Forest |
| **Height** | **Hike** |
| • 15 ft. | • 4 mi. - Moderate hike |
| **Formation** | **Road access** |
| • Cascade | • Dirt roads |
| **Elevation** | **Season** |
| • 5010 | • Spring, Summer and Fall |
| **Area** | **Latitude** |
| • Northcentral | • 47.255119 |
| **County** | **Longitude** |
| • Lewis and Clark | • -112.547143 |

### ACCESS

From Augusta drive southwest on Montana Secondary 435 for 9.4 miles to Chisolm-Barret Road. Turn left and continue for 4.1 miles to Flat Creek Road. Turn right on Flat Creek Road and drive 2.7 miles to get to the Dearborn Canyon Road. Turn right to stay on Dearborn Canyon Road. Looking straight ahead, you will see the spectacular eastern edge of the Rocky Mountains while driving 6.2 miles to the end of gravel road to the trailhead.

Bald eagle pair

## HISTORY

The Dearborn River High Bridge crosses the Dearborn River 3.5 miles southeast of Bean Lake on the Augusta-Stearns Road. It is listed on the National Register of Historic Places. Built in 1897, the bridge is an engineering classic as it is one of the last half-deck truss built bridges left remaining in the United States.

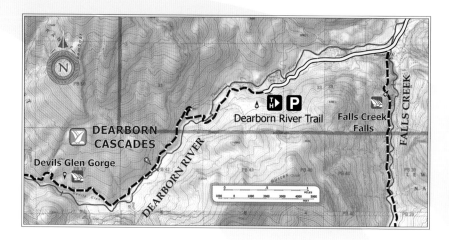

## CAMPING

**Bean Lake** is 8 miles up Flat Creek to the Dearborn Canyon road. Go west on the Dearborn Canyon 1.5 miles to the lake. Montana Fish, Wildlife, and Parks department manages this 206 acre area, which is at 4592 foot elevation. Bean Lake is a free pack in–pack out with tables, grated fire pits, two vaulted restrooms, and a seasonal boat launch.

Montana Fish, Wildlife & Parks
Parks Department
406-444-3750

## DESCRIPTION

Memorial Falls Park has a great informative kiosk to check out before you begin your hike. As you start on trail 738 you walk through a narrow canyon, where the rock formation is Neihart quartzite. This is some of the oldest and hardest sedimentary rock found in the Rocky Mountain chain. Just a short 0.25 mile hike to the falls, it nevertheless is a wonderful little hike. It has been noted that this trail can be slippery in early spring.

*Memorial Falls*

| Stream | Watershed |
|---|---|
| • Memorial Creek | • Missouri River |
| **Size** | **Forest** |
| • Small stream | • Lewis & Clark National Forest |
| **Height** | **Hike** |
| • 20 ft. | • 0.6 mi. - Easy hike |
| **Formation** | **Road access** |
| • Horsetail | • Easy highway/road access |
| **Elevation** | **Season** |
| • 6224 | • Spring, Summer and Fall |
| **Area** | **Latitude** |
| • Central | • 46.912751 |
| **County** | **Longitude** |
| • Cascade | • -110.69541 |

### ACCESS

From Neihart heading south on US Highway 89 drive 2.4 miles to Memorial Falls Park. Turn left into the parking lot and access to the trailhead.

### HISTORY

The community of Neihart was named after James L. Neihart, a miner who was among a group that discovered a drift of silver-lead ore in 1881. This find was to become one of the richest in the Little Belt Mountains. In 1882 the town of Neihart was incorporated, and presently is a recreational hot spot with Sluice Box State Park, Showdown Ski Area and Kings Hill Pass nearby.

## GEOLOGY

The igneous rock in which gold ore is found here is called pinto diorite because of its red and green spotted appearance. Sapphire mining proved profitable here, and it is estimated that more than $3 million worth of sapphires ranging in color from pale to royal blue were taken from these mines.

*Faded pictograph near Missouri River*

## CAMPING

**Many Pines Campground** (USFS), 4 miles south of Neihart, has 23 campsites. The campground has potable water, wheelchair accessible restrooms and fishing access to nearby Belt Creek.

**King's Hill Campground** (USFS, elevation 7,425') is located 9 miles south of Neihart in the Lewis and Clark National Forest. The campground has potable water and wheelchair accessible restrooms.

Lewis And Clark National Forest
1101 15th Street N.
Great Falls, MT 59401
406-791-7700

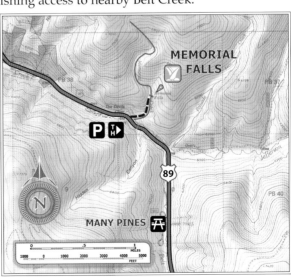

## DESCRIPTION

A dull roar and an informative sign greet you as you start walking toward the falls. This is easy, eighth-mile hike on a well marked trail. Every couple of years this section of Big Timber Creek is host to one of the wildest events in Montana, the Big Timber Race. Boaters, most being kayakers, race down the series of waterfalls and slides culminating in Big Timber Falls. The section is known for its crazy rides and high-quality bedrock whitewater.

*Upper Big Timber Falls*

SUMMARY

| Stream | Watershed |
|---|---|
| • *Big Timber Creek* | • *Yellowstone River* |
| **Size** | **Forest** |
| • *Creek* | • *Gallatin National Forest* |
| **Height** | **Hike** |
| • *120 ft.* | • *0.7 mi. - Easy hike* |
| **Formation** | **Road access** |
| • *Tiered* | • *Dirt roads* |
| **Elevation** | **Season** |
| • *6621* | • *Spring, Summer and Fall* |
| **Area** | **Latitude** |
| • *Central* | • *46.040591* |
| **County** | **Longitude** |
| • *Sweet Grass* | • *-110.24673* |

ACCESS

Drive north from Big Timber 8.1 miles on Montana Highway 191 to Wormser Loop Road. Turn left for 3.4 miles to Big Timber Canyon Road. Take another left, driving through the foothills, then into Big Timber Canyon and the majestic Crazy Mountains, proceeding for a distance of 13.3 miles to the trailhead.

*Chokecherry*

## HISTORY

The Crazy Mountains run almost 25 miles north to south, with Crazy Peak rising some 11, 214 feet high, and towering above the surrounding prairie. There are 20 some peaks above 10,000 ' elevation in this range. The Crazies are sometimes called an island range, because they look like an island in the vast prairie, though the range is 15 miles wide and 50 miles long. The area is home to many species of birds and mammals, including eagles, wild turkeys, mule deer, whitetail deer, elk , black bears, mountain lions, mountain goats, and wolverines. It's reputed to have the largest population of wolverines in the continental United States. Purportedly, the Crow Indians originally named them Crazy Woman Mountains for an early homesteader who went insane after her family was killed by native people.

*Old cabin twists with age*

## GEOLOGY

The area, some fifty million years ago, was a vast inland sea. Via fissures deep into the earth, molten rock rose through the sea's muddy bottom. Upon cooling, towering columns of igneous rock were left, then the surrounding mud and softer elements eroded away. During the last ice age some 10,000 years ago, glaciers gouged out this mountain landscape forming Montana's most impressive "island mountain" range.

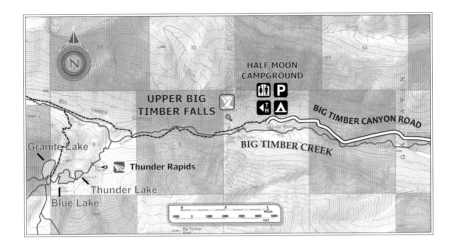

## CAMPING

**Half Moon Campground** (USFS) is another one tenth of a mile past the trailhead, at the end of Big Timber Canyon Road. This Gallatin National Forest campground is pack in–pack out; it has 12 units, 6 handicapped accessible toilets, potable water (from Memorial Day through Labor Day), and a $5/day camping fee. There is also a no-fee, day-use picnic area.

This campground does not use a reservation system; it is managed on a first-come, first-served basis. Be aware the campground may fill up on weekends and holidays during the summer months, and you should arrive in the early afternoon to ensure there is a space available for the night.

Gallatin National Forest
P.O. Box 130
Bozeman, MT 59771
406-587-6701

**Shields River Dispersed Site** is on the west side of the Crazies, 24 miles northeast of Wilsall on the Shields River Road. This is small pack in–pack out campground with only 4 campsites. There are toilet faculties, but no potable water.

## DESCRIPTION

If you have ever seen a travertine waterfall (like Mammoth Hot Springs in Yellowstone National Park), then you will recognize this falls immediately. Terraced travertine falls are very rare for Montana. Try to catch it in the spring when the water is high and the vegetation thick—it becomes a "tropical Montana hanging garden" guarded by miniature limestone caves.

*Warm Springs Creek Falls*

## SUMMARY

| Stream | Watershed |
|---|---|
| • Warm Springs Creek | • Clark Fork River |
| **Size** | **Forest** |
| • Small stream | • Helena National Forest |
| **Height** | **Hike** |
| • 34 ft. | • 0.5 mi. - short walk from road |
| **Formation** | **Road access** |
| • Terraced | • Dirt roads |
| **Elevation** | **Season** |
| • 4806 | • Spring, Summer and Fall |
| **Area** | **Latitude** |
| • Central | • 46.598274 |
| **County** | **Longitude** |
| • Powell | • -112.787613 |

### ACCESS

From Garrison travel north I-90 W for 3.0 miles to Exit 170 (Phosphate exit). From the off ramp, take a sharp right onto Brock Creek Road for 1.1 miles to Warm Springs Creek Road. Take a left onto Warm Springs Creek Road (FR 106), driving up 4.5 miles to a small pullout on the right. Take the undeveloped trail leading to the falls from the small pullout parking area.

*Elkhorn cabin*

## HISTORY

Montana's first gold strikes were in this area, which boasts the ghost towns of Gold Creek (founded in 1857 at Montana's first strike) and, to its south, Pioneer City (1867). Located off I-90 Exit 166 (Gold Creek exit) in the Flint Creek Range, each has a few remnant cabins surviving today.

*Garnet ghost town*

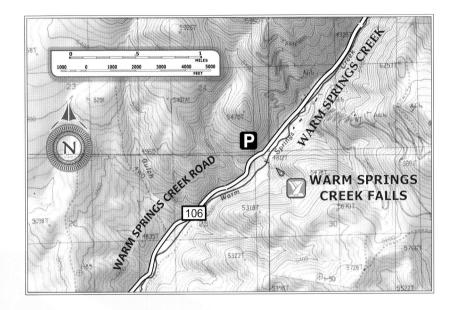

WARM SPRINGS CREEK FALLS

## CAMPING

**Cromwell Dixon Campground** (USFS, elevation 6,260′) is 27 miles east of Garrison on Montana Highway 12. This campground is open from Memorial Day weekend through Labor Day weekend. There are 15 campsites, potable water and vault toilets. Cromwell Dixon offers truly scenic vistas and access to the Continental Divide Trail, and is named for the first man to fly an "aeroplane" across any part of the Divide, in 1911. The fee is $8.00 per night.

Helena National Forest
2880 Skyway Drive
Helena, MT 59602
406-449-5201

**Racetrack Creek Campground and Picnic Area** (USFS) is located 12.5 miles west of Interstate 90. This is a pack in–pack out campground with 13 campsites and access to a rushing Racetrack Creek. There are potable water, vault toilets and a 16-day stay limit at this campground. There is no fee for camping at this campground.

Beaverhead–Deerlodge National Forest
420 Barrett Street
Dillion, MT 59725-3572
406-683-3900

# Montana Waterfalls Southcentral Region

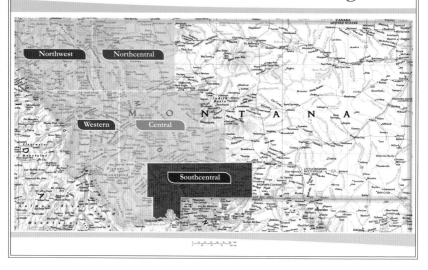

## DESCRIPTION

From the trailhead for TR 18 you start your hike walking parallel with the magnificent Boulder River for about 1/4 of a mile. Abruptly you start to climb out of the valley up the mountainside and soon you cross the Absaroka–Beartooth Wilderness boundary. The trail becomes somewhat rocky and has a few switchbacks offering some incredible views of the Absarokas. After hiking 1.5 miles up Great Falls Creek trail, you want to take the undeveloped trail to the left. This will take you down a steep draw some 200 yards to a very cool Great Falls Creek Falls.

*Great Falls Creek Falls*

SUMMARY

| Stream | Watershed |
|---|---|
| • Great Falls Creek | • Yellowstone River |
| **Size** | **Forest** |
| • Creek | • Gallatin National Forest |
| **Height** | **Hike** |
| • 20 ft. | • 2.9 mi. - Easy hike |
| **Formation** | **Road access** |
| • Horsetail | • Dirt roads |
| **Elevation** | **Season** |
| • 6709 | • Spring, Summer and Fall |
| **Area** | **Latitude** |
| • Southcentral | • 45.462117 |
| **County** | **Longitude** |
| • Park | • -110.221882 |

ACCESS

Drive south from Big Timber on Montana Secondary 298, past historic McLeod, 27.51 miles to the Main Boulder Road (FR 6639). Continue going south another 3.3 miles to the turnoff for trail 18 (Great Falls Creek trail) and the subsequent parking lot.

*Boulder River near falls*

## HISTORY

The headwaters of the Boulder River are in the Absaroka Mountains deep in the Absaroka–Beartooth Wilderness Area. From there the stream flows pretty much due north through the spectacular Boulder Valley, where it joins the Yellowstone River at the town of Big Timber.

Natural and man-made wonders can be found all along this valley. Hiking out of the historic Main Boulder Ranger Station, you can view Lions Head, a prominent rock outcropping, and Paleo-Indian caves. Almost to the end of the Main Boulder Road is Box Canyon Road, leading to the mining ghost town of Independence 5 miles away. The town's heyday was during the 1890s, and then it was mostly abandoned. Today you can view the historic ruins from the road, but the site is privately owned, so please don't trespass.

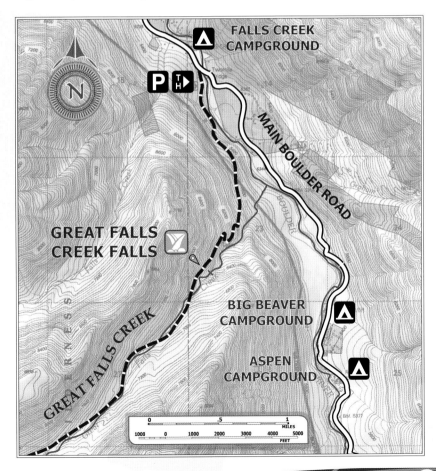

## CAMPING

**Falls Creek Campground** (USFS) is 3 miles south of Natural Bridges State Monument on the Main Boulder Road (County Road 212). Located in the Gallatin National Forest, this campground is run by the U.S. Forest Service. It is a pack in–pack out, tents-only campground with 8 campsites. There are handicapped accessible toilets, potable water from Memorial Day to Labor Day, and there is no camping fee.

Big Beaver Campground is a USFS camping area 3 miles farther south from Falls CG on County Road 212 (access road not suitable for vehicles longer than 32 feet). There are 5 campsites, pack in–pack out, no water, handicapped accessible toilets, and no camping fee.

**Aspen Campground** (USFS) is a beautiful aspen- and evergreen-forested campground adjacent to the Boulder River, 33.5 miles south of Big Timber. There are 8 campsites, potable water from Memorial Day to Labor Day and a handicapped accessible vault toilet. There also are some bear-proof storage containers. This is a first-come, first-served campground with a $5.00/day camping fee.

**Chippy Park Campground** (USFS) 34.5 miles south of Big Timber is another first-come, first-served campground with 7 campsites and 2 walk-in sites. There are a handicapped accessible vault toilet, potable water from Memorial Day to Labor Day, and a $5.00/day fee.

Gallatin National Forest
P.O. Box 130
Bozeman, MT 59771
406-587-6701

## DESCRIPTION

This is a very popular trailhead with parking and handicapped facilities at the end of Hyalite Creek Road. Hyalite Creek runs adjacent to the 1.5-mile trail to Grotto Falls. This trail is wheelchair accessible, allowing persons with disabilities to be able to view the very scenic Grotto Falls. Rustic log benches also have been placed in picturesque spots along the trail. Trail 427 continues past Grotto Falls up the "Valley of the Falls" to Hyalite Lake and eventually connects to the Gallatin Divide–Devils Backbone trail on Hyalite Peak (10,298').

Valley of the Falls is the name we have given to this rugged, splendorous valley running north to south going up Hyalite Creek. There are 11 waterfalls that you can see or hike to off of TR 427. From Grotto Falls to Sil Vous Plait Falls, the Valley of the Falls hike offers views that everyone should see. Here are the falls and their elevations: Grotto Falls 7,728', Twin Falls 8,461', Arch Falls 7,405', Silken Skein Falls 8,159', Maid of the Mist Falls 7,743', Champagne Falls 7,864', Chasm Falls 7,966, Shower Falls 8,235', Apex Falls 8,399, Alpine Falls 8,862' and Sil Vous Plait Falls 8,875.

*Grotto Falls*

SUMMARY

| Stream | Watershed |
|--------|-----------|
| • Hyalite Creek | • Missouri River |
| **Size** | **Forest** |
| • Creek | • Gallatin National Forest |
| **Height** | **Hike** |
| • 60 ft. | • 3.0 mi. - Easy hike |
| **Formation** | **Road access** |
| • Terraced | • Dirt roads |
| **Elevation** | **Season** |
| • 7228 | • Summer and Fall |
| **Area** | **Latitude** |
| • Southcentral | • 48.565589 |
| **County** | **Longitude** |
| • Gallatin | • -114.682975 |

## ACCESS

From Bozeman drive south on 19th Street 7.1 miles to Hyalite
Canyon Road. Turn left and go south on Hyalite Canyon road 11.4
miles to Forest Road 62. Take a right and drive south 2.3 miles to the
end of the road and the trailhead.

*Silvery lupine*

## HISTORY

History Rock trailhead is 10 miles up Hyalite Canyon Road (FR 62). One mile before Hyalite Reservoir, find a pull-off on the right side of the road and park. About 1.2 miles up this trail is a sandstone rock that was supposedly etched by the famous Lewis and Clark Expedition member and frontiersman, John Colter. This trail continues another mile to the divide, past Fox Meadow known for its beautiful wildflower displays, and a view of the South Cottonwood Creek drainage.

Hyalite Canyon also has some of the best ice climbing in the continental U.S. This area is known for its early-forming and accessible ice, with some ice forming in late November and usually lasting till March or sometimes April. The canyon has over 70 ice climbs ranging from beginners' to those that, once done, haven't been repeated. Ice climbing is a serious technical sport; it should not be attempted by anyone without sufficient experience. Hiring a guide for this extreme sport is advisable.

*Champange Falls*

*Chasm Falls*

## CAMPING

**Chisholm Campground** (USFS) is at the end of Hyalite Reservoir with another great view of the Hyalites. There are 10 units, with handicapped accessible toilets, drinking water, trash pickup, $10/day fee and a two-week maximum stay. There are additional-vehicle cost and firewood fee.

**Hood Creek campground** (USFS), 17 miles south on Hyalite Canyon Road, overlooks scenic Hyalite Reservoir and the rugged Hyalite Mountains. There are 18 units, with handicapped accessible toilets, water, trash pickup, $10/day fee and a maximum stay of two weeks. There are additional-vehicle cost and firewood fee.

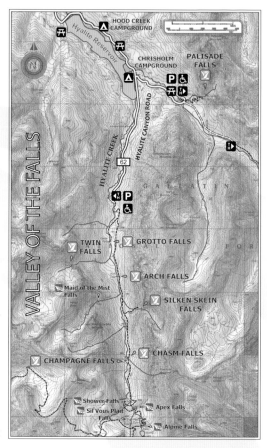

**Langhor Campground** (USFS) is 11 miles south of Bozeman on Hyalite Canyon Road. This nice campground sits adjacent to sparkling Hyalite Creek. It's open from May 15 to September 15, has 10 campsites, handicapped accessible facilities (toilet, fishing, 2 sites and trail). There is an $11.00/day camping fee, an additional-vehicle fee of $7.00/day, with the maximum stay of two weeks.

Gallatin National Forest
P.O. Box 130
Bozeman, MT 59771
406-587-6701

# Natural Bridge Falls

## DESCRIPTION

The trailhead starts at the parking lot and splits in a very short distance. The trail to the left stays on the north side of the river, the trail to the right crosses the Boulder River via a sturdily built wooden footbridge. The view from the bridge allows you to see the river disappearing underground into a cavernous hole. Some 200 feet away and below the river, a rock face juts 30 feet into a large clear pool. There is handicapped accessibility to certain falls viewing points.

*Natural Bridge Falls*

SUMMARY

| Stream | Watershed |
|---|---|
| • Boulder River | • Yellowstone River |
| **Size** | **Forest** |
| • River | • Gallatin National Forest |
| **Height** | **Hike** |
| • 80 ft. | • 1.5 mi. - short walk from road |
| **Formation** | **Road access** |
| • Punchbowl | • Dirt roads |
| **Elevation** | **Season** |
| • 5194 | • Spring, Summer and Fall |
| **Area** | **Latitude** |
| • Southcentral | • 45.548829 |
| **County** | **Longitude** |
| • Sweet Grass | • -110.206518 |

ACCESS
Drive south of Big Timber on Montana Secondary 298, past the historic town of McLeod, 25.1 miles to Natural Bridge State Monument.

*Absaroka Beartooth Wilderness sign*

## HISTORY

The headwaters of the Boulder River are in the Absaroka Mountains deep in the Absaroka–Beartooth Wilderness Area. From there it flows pretty much due north through the spectacular Boulder Valley, where it joins the Yellowstone River at the town of Big Timber.

Natural and man-made wonders can be seen all along this valley. Hiking out of the historic Main Boulder Ranger Station, you can view Lions Head, a prominent rock outcropping, and Paleo-Indian caves. Almost to the end of the Main Boulder Road is Box Canyon Road, which leads to the mining ghost town of Independence 5 miles away. The town's brief mining heyday was during the 1890s, after which it was for the most part abandoned. Today you can view the historic ruins from the road—but the town is privately owned, so please don't trespass.

*Historic Main Boulder Ranger Station*

## CAMPING

**Falls Creek Campground** (USFS) is 3 miles south of Natural Bridge State Monument on the Main Boulder Road (County Road 212). Located in the Gallatin National Forest, this campground is a pack in–pack out, tents-only location with 8 campsites. There are handicapped accessible toilets, potable water from Memorial Day to Labor Day, and there is no camping fee.

**Big Beaver Campground** (USFS) is a camping area 3 miles farther south from Falls Creek Campground on County Road 212 (access road not suitable for vehicles longer than 32 feet). There are 5 campsites, pack in–pack out, no water, handicapped accessible toilets, and no camping fee.

Gallatin National Forest
P.O. Box 130
Bozeman, MT 59771
406-587-6701

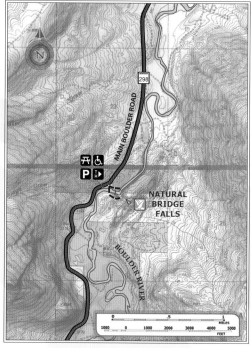

## DESCRIPTION

The trailhead starts from Ousel Falls Park parking lot. At the starting point for the trail are a handicapped accessible toilet and a highly informative interpretive sign. Hiking down on the well maintained, switch-backing trail into this wonderful canyon is fun. At the bottom is a sturdy footbridge crossing the South Fork of the West Fork of the Gallatin River. Walking upstream among towering Engelmann spruce trees you soon hear, then see, South Fork Cascade. A picnic table is there for hikers to stop to rest, enjoy the view and eat if they like. Continuing upstream along this forested trail another 400 yards is dazzling Ousel Falls. Another picnic table is located at this lush, mossy, enchanted canyon-floor setting for you to enjoy.

*Ousel Falls*

SUMMARY

| Stream | Watershed |
|---|---|
| • *South Fork of the West Fork of the Gallatin River* | • *Gallatin River* |
| **Size** | **Forest** |
| • *Creek* | • *Gallatin National Forest* |
| **Height** | **Hike** |
| • *55 ft.* | • *1.6 mi. - Easy hike* |
| **Formation** | **Road access** |
| • *Tiered* | • *Easy highway/road access* |
| **Elevation** | **Season** |
| • *6637* | • *All* |
| **Area** | **Latitude** |
| • *Southcentral* | • *45.238847* |
| **County** | **Longitude** |
| • *Gallatin* | • *-111.341543* |

## ACCESS

From Bozeman, drive west on Huffine Lane 6.7 miles to Four Corners. Turn south on US Highway 191 for another 33.9 miles. You cross the beautiful Gallatin River many times and view some of Montana's finest scenery in the Gallatin Canyon, before the turnoff to the Big Sky Road. Take a right, driving west 2.9 miles to Ousel Falls Road. At the junction before you turn left, straight ahead you can't help but notice awesome Lone Mountain, home to Big Sky ski resort and one of the highest peaks in the Gallatin National Forest at 11,188'. At Ousel Falls Road go left for another 2 miles to Ousel Falls Park and the trailheads at the back of the parking lot.

*Bighorn ram in the Madison Range*

## HISTORY

Ousel Falls, we believe, is named after a bird, the water ouzel, or the American dipper as it is more commonly known in other areas of the United States. Water ouzels are often spotted in the water and along the banks upstream and downstream of Ousel Falls. They feed on insect life in streams; in deeper water they actually dive and run along the bottom with half-open wings.

Big Sky community sits at the base of 11,188′ Lone Mountain. This area was first homesteaded in 1915 by Clarence Lytel as a working cattle ranch he named the Lone Mountain Ranch. In 1926 it was then sold to Chicago paper mill tycoon F.O. Butler, who had built many of the existing buildings on

*Old homestead on Gallatin River*

the ranch. In the late 1960s Chet Huntley, with Chrysler and several other corporations, purchased the Lone Mountain Ranch and other land, much of which now is known as Big Sky. Big Sky Mountain and Meadows Villages in the early 1970s started developing into one of Montana's first destination alpine-ski areas. Today the Big Sky resort has over 3,500 ski-able acres and, with 4,100′ of total vertical drop, ranks as one of the U.S. ski areas with the most vertical drop.

## GEOLOGY

The Spanish Peaks massif parallels the western side of the Gallatin Canyon. This 3-billion-year-old metamorphic rock is some of the oldest in North America. From the mouth of the canyon to the locality

of Big Sky these rugged mountains are huge blocks of Precambrian basement rock uplifted along the Spanish Peaks fault. Going south from the fault, toward Yellowstone National Park, you see more sedimentary formations deposited during the Paleozoic period.

*Ousel Falls Park*

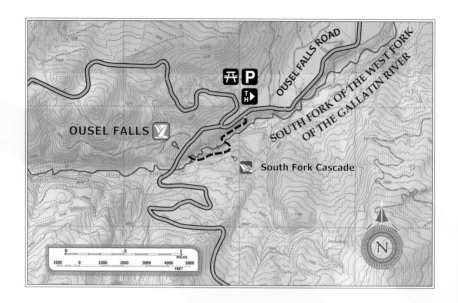

## CAMPING

**Greek Creek Campground** (USFS) is 31 miles south of Bozeman on US Highway 191. Available from May 15 to September 15 are 14 units, potable water, handicapped accessible facilities, and trash pickup, for a $10/day site fee with a $6/day additional-vehicle fee. Campers enjoy scenery and wildlife viewing, fishing, hiking, kayaking, and rafting.

**Moose Creek Flat Campground** (USFS) is 32 miles south of Bozeman on US Highway 191. Available from May 15 to September 15, there are 12 units plus 1 group site, potable water, trash pickup. Fees $10/day, plus $6/day for each additional vehicle. The Gallatin River offers blue-ribbon trout fishing, hiking, rafting, and kayaking. Wildflower viewing is excellent in season.

Gallatin National Forest
P.O. Box 130
Bozeman, MT 59771
406-587-6701

## DESCRIPTION

The trailhead starts out of the Palisades Falls Picnic Area parking lot. Palisades Falls National Recreation trail is a short, 0.8 mile asphalt-coated surface to a beautiful 80′ waterfall. You are walking through towering Engelmann spruce and red fir as you switch back up to the base of the volcanic cliffs. Palisades Falls cascades over an ancient lava flow, complete with massive hexagonal basalt columns. There are interpretive exhibits in both Braille and English. The trail's maximum grade is 11%, which is the most difficult classification for handicapped use.

*Palisades Falls*

SUMMARY

| Stream | Watershed |
|--------|-----------|
| • *Palisades Creek* | • *Gallatin River* |
| **Size** | **Forest** |
| • *Small stream* | • *Gallatin National Forest* |
| **Height** | **Hike** |
| • *125 ft.* | • *1.7 mi. - Easy hike* |
| **Formation** | **Road access** |
| • *Horsetail* | • *Rough roads at times* |
| **Elevation** | **Season** |
| • *7320* | • *Spring and Summer* |
| **Area** | **Latitude** |
| • *Southcentral* | • *45.468679* |
| **County** | **Longitude** |
| • *Gallatin* | • *-110.939641* |

### ACCESS

From Bozeman drive south on 19th Street, 7.1 miles to Hyalite Canyon Road. Go south on Hyalite Canyon Road 10.5 miles to FR 62. Continue on FR 62 for 1.2 miles to FR 3163. Turn left onto FR 3163 for 1.1 miles to Palisades Falls Picnic Area and trailhead.

### HISTORY

History Rock trailhead is 10 miles up Hyalite Canyon Road (FR 62), one mile before Hyalite Reservoir, with the pull-off to the right. About 1.2 miles up this trail is a sandstone rock that was supposedly etched by the Lewis and Clark Expedition member and frontiersman John Colter. This trail continues another mile to the divide, past Fox Meadow (known for its beautiful wildflower displays), and a view of the South Cottonwood Creek drainage.

Hyalite Canyon also has some of the best ice climbing in the continental U.S. This area is known for its early-forming and accessible ice, with some ice forming in late November and usually lasting until

March or even April. The canyon has more than 70 ice climbs, ranging from beginner to those that, once achieved, haven't ever been repeated. Ice climbing is a serious technical sport; it should not be attempted by anyone without sufficient experience. Hiring a guide for this extreme sport is advisable.

## CAMPING

**Palisades Falls Picnic Area** is a nice 4-unit picnic area with no water, a handicapped accessible toilet, and no fees. There are two Gallatin National Forest campgrounds close to Palisades Falls.

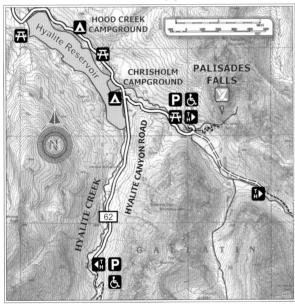

**Hood Creek Campground** (USFS), 17 miles south on Hyalite Canyon Road, overlooks scenic Hyalite Reservoir and the rugged Hyalite Mountains. There are 18 units, with handicapped accessible toilets, water, trash pick-up, $10/day fee and a maximum stay of two weeks. Additional vehicle cost and firewood fee.

**Chisholm Campground** (USFS) is at the end of Hyalite Reservoir with another great view of the Hyalites. There are 10 units, with handicapped accessible toilets, drinking water, trash pickup, $10/day fee and a two-week maximum stay. Additional vehicle cost and firewood fee.

Gallatin National Forest
P.O. Box 130
Bozeman, MT 59771
406-587-6701

## DESCRIPTION

From the trailhead (TR47) at the campground, Pine Creek Falls is a mile up Pine Creek Trail. The trail can be rocky and steep in places, but offers one truly enjoyable hike. This is a popular, scenic trail that also leads to alpine Jewel Lake and Pine Creek Lake at 9,000'-plus elevation, situated in a glacial basin.

*Pine Creek Falls*

SUMMARY

| | |
|---|---|
| **Stream**<br>• Pine Creek | **Watershed**<br>• Yellowstone River |
| **Size**<br>• Creek | **Forest**<br>• Gallatin National Forest |
| **Height**<br>• 100 ft. | **Hike**<br>• 2.5 mi. - Moderate hike |
| **Formation**<br>• Shoestring | **Road access**<br>• Easy highway/road access |
| **Elevation**<br>• 6467 | **Season**<br>• Spring, Summer and Fall |
| **Area**<br>• Southcentral | **Latitude**<br>• 45.489652 |
| **County**<br>• Park | **Longitude**<br>• -110.498686 |

## ACCESS

From Livingston drive south on US Highway 89 down through the Paradise Valley along the Yellowstone River, 2.9 miles to East River Road. Turn left on Montana Secondary 540 (East River Road) and drive 7.8 miles to Luccock Park Road (FR 202). This road will wind another 2.7 miles up beautifully forested hillside to Pine Creek Campground.

*Common harebell*

## HISTORY

Paradise Valley extends 50 miles, from the north end at the historic railroad town of Livingston to the south end at Gardiner and the entrance to Yellowstone National Park. Running adjacent to the valley are the Absaroka-Beartooth Mountains to the east and Hyalite Mountains to the west, with the blue-ribbon-fishing Yellowstone River winding down the middle. Yellowstone National Park, on March 1, 1872, became the world's first national park. This was done by an order signed by President Ulysses S. Grant, which set aside 2.2 million acres of wilderness "as a public park or a pleasuring ground for the benefit and enjoyment of the people".

The first white explorers into the Yellowstone country were a few members of the Lewis and Clark Expedition led by William Clark on the return trip in 1806. One of the group's soldiers was John Colter. At Fort Mandan (North Dakota) in August of 1806 he requested and received an early release from the army, and returned upstream with two trappers heading to the upper Missouri. He is credited for being the first frontiersman to enter and describe the greater Yellowstone Park area. When few whites believed his description of the area with geysers and other geophysical phenomena, they disparaged it as "Colter's Hell."

*Pine Creek beauty*

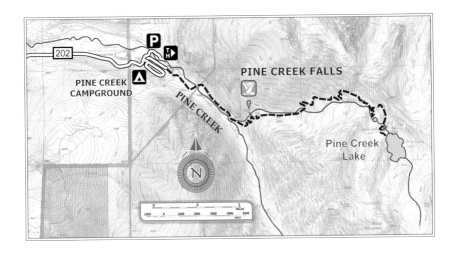

## CAMPING

**Pine Creek Campground** (USFS) sits at an elevation of 5,500' and is located at the western end of the Absaroka Mountains in the Gallatin National Forest. There are 25 camping units plus one group-reservation-only site, handicapped accessible facilities, drinking water, trash pickup and a $10/day fee. An additional $6/day fee is charged for each additional vehicle (2 maximum). Besides the scenic views, there are hiking trails including some with access to the Absaroka¬Beartooth Wilderness Area.

Gallatin National Forest
P.O. Box 130
Bozeman, MT 59771
406-587-6701

*Pine Creek Campground*

# Stillwater River Cascades

## DESCRIPTION

From the trailhead for TR 24, you will hike only about 300 yards or so, crossing just into the Absaroka–Beartooth Wilderness Area boundary when you reach these powerful cascades. The river here cuts through broken granite within a nearly sheer-walled gorge to create a series of rugged drops. The views are unbelievable and well worth the short hike.

*Stillwater Cascades from the bottom*

## SUMMARY

| | |
|---|---|
| **Stream**<br>• *Stillwater River* | **Watershed**<br>• *Yellowstone River* |
| **Size**<br>• *River* | **Forest**<br>• *Custer National Forest* |
| **Height**<br>• *150 ft.* | **Hike**<br>• *1.5 mi. - Easy hike* |
| **Formation**<br>• *Cascade* | **Road access**<br>• *Dirt roads* |
| **Elevation**<br>• *5400* | **Season**<br>• *Spring, Summer and Fall* |
| **Area**<br>• *Southcentral* | **Latitude**<br>• *45.347902* |
| **County**<br>• *Stillwater* | **Longitude**<br>• *-109.900832* |

## ACCESS

From Absarokee, travel south on Montana Highway 78 for 2.3 miles to Montana Secondary 419 (Nye Road). Turn right onto Montana Secondary 419 and drive to its end some 28.5 miles to the the trailhead for TR 24.

## HISTORY

Granite Peak, at 12,799', is the tallest mountain in the state of Montana. It is located in the Beartooth Mountains in south-central Montana next to the Wyoming border. The Beartooths are part of the Beartooth Plateau, the largest high-elevation plateau in the United States. Here are more than 25 mountain peaks that surpass 12,000' or more. Around 25 smaller glaciers exist in the Beartooths along with some 300 beautiful lakes.

Trappers came into the region in the early 1830s. Legendary frontiersmen including Jim Bridger, John Colter, Joseph Dixon, Jedediah Smith, George Drouillard and others created lasting reputations for themselves in the mountain man tradition. Colter's incredible exploits led to the discovery of today's Yellowstone National Park area.

*Stillwater Cascades from the top*

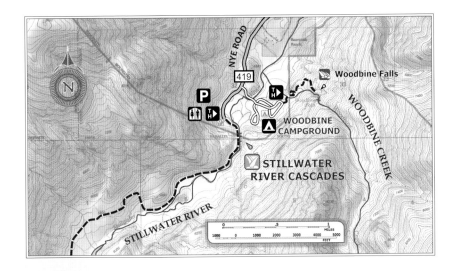

## CAMPING

**Woodbine Campground** (USFS, elevation 5,060') has 44 campsites, handicapped accessible toilet, potable water, corral and hitching post at trailhead. Fee is $20/day, with 10-day-stay limit.

**Old Nye Campground** (USFS) is a small pack in–pack out recreation site that has only 6 campsites. Toilet facilities are available. There is no fee for this campground.

Custer National Forest
1310 Main Street
Billings, MT 59105
406-657-6200

## DESCRIPTION

Woodbine Falls Trail starts in the northeast corner of Woodbine Campground. From the trailhead you begin to climb uphill gradually, but in just a couple of hundred yards the trail gets more difficult by switchbacking up the mountainside. Although it's only 0.75 mile up the trail to Woodbine Falls, you climb 564' in elevation. The falls is a magnificent display of cascades, vertical falls and boulder drops. The views are spectacular from the final overlook.

*Woodbine Falls upper portion*

## SUMMARY

| | |
|---|---|
| **Stream**<br>• Woodbine Creek | **Watershed**<br>• Yellowstone River |
| **Size**<br>• Creek | **Forest**<br>• Custer National Forest |
| **Height**<br>• 134 ft. | **Hike**<br>• 1.5 mi. - moderate hike |
| **Formation**<br>• Shoestring | **Road access**<br>• Dirt roads |
| **Elevation**<br>• 5866 | **Season**<br>• Spring, Summer and Fall |
| **Area**<br>• Southcentral | **Latitude**<br>• 45.35305 |
| **County**<br>• Stillwater | **Longitude**<br>• -119.885426 |

### ACCESS

From Fishtail, head southwest on FR 419 (Nye Road) for 24.8 miles to the Woodbine Campground turnoff. Turn left into Woodbine Campground and drive 0.2 mile to the southeast corner to the trailhead for TR 93.

## HISTORY

The Absaroka–Beartooth Wilderness was established in 1975 from national forest land located in Montana and Wyoming. The Absaroka Range and the Beartooth Range encompass this 944,000-acre wilderness area. Parts of three national forests — Custer, Gallatin and Shoshone — make up an expansive alpine paradise. Granite Peak (12,799′ elevation), which is the tallest mountain in Montana, and Francs Peak (13,185′ elevation) in Wyoming are the tallest peaks in the wilderness, which has 30 peaks rising above 12,000′ elevation.

The Bozeman Trail is listed on the National Register of Historic Places. The trail originated as a route for gold miners into Montana's gold rush territory. Jim Bridger purportedly blazed the trail connecting the Oregon Trail in Wyoming to Virginia City, Montana in June 1864, and was followed a few months later by John Bozeman and John Jacobs leading the first wagon train full of miners and settlers along the new route. The Bozeman Trail came down Red Lodge Creek, crossing over to Butcher Creek, then continued to the Rosebud Creek drainage. The trail crossed Rosebud Creek below the confluence of East Rosebud Creek and West Rosebud Creek, then headed northwest to cross the Stillwater River before angling toward Bozeman Pass.

*Woodbine Falls lower portion*

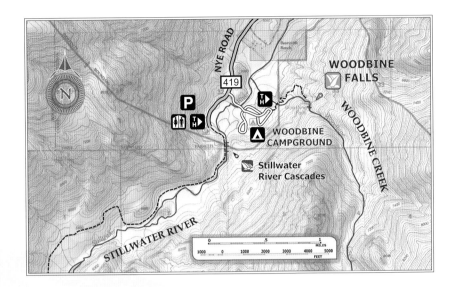

## CAMPING

**Woodbine Campground** (USFS, elevation 5,060') has 44 campsites, $20/day fee, with 10 days maximum stay, handicapped accessible toilet, potable water, corral and hitching post at trailhead.

**Old Nye Campground** (USFS) is a small pack in–pack out recreation site that has only 6 campsites. Toilet facilities are available. There is no fee for this campground.

Custer National Forest
1310 Main Street
Billings, MT 59105
406-657-6200

# LEAVE NO TRACE

Leave No Trace is an international organization dedicated to helping the outdoor recreationist minimize their impact on nature through their seven principles and their educationsal programs.

- Plan ahead and prepare

- Travel and camp on durable surfaces

- Dispose of waste properly

- Leave what you find

- Minimize campfire impacts

- Respect wildlife

- Be considerate of other visitors

The Leave No Trace Seven Principles have been reprinted with the permission of the Leave No Trace Center for Outdoor Ehtics: www.LNT.org

# ABOUT THE AUTHORS

*Waterfall explorers at Martin Falls. Back row, right to left: Nathan Johnson, Larry Johnson, and Maria Elena Johnson; front row, right to left: Cameron Fisher and Tristan Redearth*

## NATHAN JOHNSON

Nathan Johnson, born and raised in Montana, currently enjoys residing in the mountainous western region of the state. There he spends way too much time bushwhacking in search of waterfalls, hunting for waterslides to kayak, and spending generally unreasonable drawn-out moments wandering through wild areas. His son Tristan often accompanies him on these excursions, resulting in the sometimes rare 'father-son bonding time' that we all strive for. Sometimes Nathan is also found rock hounding, gold panning, feverishly stomping up hillsides in search of boulders to climb (or just sit by), darning socks, tinkering with wheelchair motors, pondering awkward art projects, feeding lizards on an irregular basis, reading burned books, praying at the last moment, giving away ski boots, and imitating goats.

## LARRY JOHNSON

Larry has spent the majority of his years hiking, living, and working in Montana. He currently resides in Helena with his wife Maria.

To contact the authors, please visit their website www.waterfallsmontana.com.